I was excited to read *Made to Crave* but never did I think it would change my outlook on eating habits and, really, my relationship with God. Each chapter I read was just what I needed. . . . In just six weeks I lost seventeen pounds. But the gain in my relationship with God has been far greater than my weight loss! It amazed me — as God always does — that He made me to CRAVE HIM, not the things in life that I had been craving. Since the study I am reading the Word or something in regards to God all the time. — JANE D.

This book has shown me if I would just rely on God to help me through my struggles, they might not feel as difficult. The other big thing *Made to Crave* has shown me is that, with God's help, I can do things that I would not be able to do on my own. I'm trying to run now, which I've never been able to do. I really believe I will be able to run. I've never believed that before. Thank you! — DENISE L.

I started this journey weighing 316 pounds and so far have lost fourteen. Although I have a long way to go, I'm definitely focusing less on food and have been making wiser food choices. Somedays are easier than others, and I have to remember that my body is not my own and that I need to honor God with the way I choose to treat it. But as long as I continue to stay focused, I know I can be victorious this time around. — MELISSA S.

I had always been a picky eater growing up and ate way too much junk food. I wanted to take back my body and start eating right, especially now that I am getting older and need to be more cautious about what I eat. *Made to Crave* is not about weight loss; it is about complete dependence on God. It is a lifestyle change that is meant to continue even when the book is closed and back on the shelf. Because of this book I have made progress with reaching my goal of being a healthier person.... I know I am on the right track! —KIRSTEN W.

•

For me this journey hasn't been as much about food as it has been about understanding why I compromise. Food is just one area that I stink at listening to God and following through. In my twenties I had many destructive food issues. I barely ate and when I did, I purged. The cycle of guilt and shame, mixed with times of successful moderation, was still a roller coaster I found myself on after all these years. Thoughts about food dominated my mind instead of deep communion with God. Now, since I started reading *Made to Crave*, God is using this journey to shake me up and to ultimately free me. This book has made me feel such peace and protection in God's gentle conviction. Today, I feel empowered and victorious with a new resolve to head north and stop compromising. —LISA S.

MADE TO
CRAVE

SATISFYING YOUR DEEPEST DESIRE
WITH GOD, NOT FOOD

LYSA TERKEURST
President of Proverbs 31 Ministries

ZONDERVAN

ZONDERVAN.com/
AUTHORTRACKER
follow your favorite authors

ZONDERVAN

Made to Crave
Copyright © 2010 by Lysa TerKeurst

This title is also available as a Zondervan ebook. Visit www.zondervan.com/ebooks.

This title is also available in a Zondervan audio edition. Visit www.zondervan.fm.

Requests for information should be addressed to:

Zondervan, *Grand Rapids, Michigan 49530*

Library of Congress Cataloging-in-Publication Data

TerKeurst, Lysa.
        Made to crave : satisfying your deepest desire with God, not food / Lysa
TerKeurst.
            p.   cm.
        ISBN   978-0-310-29326-2 (softcover)
        1. Christian women—Religious life. 2. God (Christianity)—Worship and love.
    3. Spirituality. 4. Food—Religious aspects—Christianity. I. Title.
    BV4527.T4625   2010
    248.8'43—dc22   2010028323

Any Internet addresses (websites, blogs, etc.) and telephone numbers in this book are offered as a resource. They are not intended in any way to be or imply an endorsement by Zondervan, nor does Zondervan vouch for the content of these sites and numbers for the life of this book.

Published in association with the literary agency of Fedd & Company, Inc., Post Office Box 34973, Austin, TX 78734.

Cover design: Curt Diepenhorst
Cover photography: Getty Image®
Interior design: Beth Shagene

Printed in the United States of America

11 12 13 14 15 /DCI/ 34 33 32 31 30 29 28 27 26 25 24 23 22 21 20 19 18 17 16

This book is dedicated to you, my friend.
While I don't know your name, God does.
I believe He led you to pick up this book because
He wants you to know your issues with food
are not a curse but a gateway through which
He can touch the rawest places of your heart and
help you discover a deep satisfaction only He can give.
Go ahead and dare to believe that this time
around things will be different.

Contents

Acknowledgments

To Art: Thank you for never letting me settle with my health. And thank you for loving me despite the fact that I've asked you a thousand times if my backside looks big. I love the way you always say, "No." But it still cracks me up that the first song on your iPod is, "Fat Bottomed Girls, You Make the Rockin' World Go 'Round." I love you forever.

To my five priority blessings ... Jackson, Mark, Hope, Ashley, and Brooke: May you always crave God more. I love you so very, very much.

To Holly: I could never have taken this journey without you. Words cannot express the depth of my appreciation for you. Thank you for processing every word of this book during our morning runs.

To Marybeth: Thank you for spending hours on the phone assuring me that if you could do this, I could too.

To LeAnn: Thank you for not kicking me out of your office when I asked you to join me on this journey. You inspire me! Your love for me and this ministry is something I thank God for every day.

To Karen: I love being one of your three strands. You can do it, girl!

To the staff and ministry teams of Proverbs 31 Ministries: There is no other group of women with whom I would want to do life and ministry. It is an honor to know you.

To Rob and Ashley Eagar: I will forever be indebted to your commitment to excellence. Thank you for pushing me to reach deeper, strive higher, and never settle for less.

To Esther Fedorkevich: You are so much more than an agent; you're one of my best friends. Thank you for believing in this message even when I was convinced only three people in the world would ever want to read it.

To Moe, Sandy, Dudley, Don, Alicia, Robin, Greg, T.J., Karen, and the rest of the Zondervan team: This book would not be what it is without your expertise and commitment. Thank you for so clearly catching the vision of my message.

And, finally, to my "In the Loop Group" and special blog friends who walked through the early drafts of this message: Thank you for your feedback, your encouragement, and the amazing testimonies you sent in reminding me why the message of *Made to Crave* is a needed one.

Finding Your "Want To"

A typical book on healthy lifestyle choices should contain lots of talk on vegetables, calories, colon cleanses, and phrases like "you must," "you should," "or else."

I have a problem with all that talk. I know most of it. It's not the "how to" I'm missing. It's the "want to" … really wanting to make changes and deciding that the results of those changes are worth the sacrifice. More than once, I've stood in the aisle at Walmart holding said typical book in one hand with my other hand wedged into the back pocket of my jeans. Jeans, I should add, I wished were several sizes smaller.

It's not the "how to" I'm missing. It's the "want to" … really wanting to make changes and deciding that the results of those changes are worth the sacrifice.

While I stood there looking at the healthy eating book, a shopping cart full of things I felt I could not live without stared back at me. Indeed, that cart mocked me. Part of me hated the junk food in that cart; but another part of me—a bigger part, evidently—loved the junk food in that cart. So, I'd return the book to the shelf, toss my head back, and think, "Another day, another time. I'm doing the best I can."

In light of this admission, I think it only appropriate to be honest with you about a few things right up front.

1. I am emotionally allergic to typical books on healthy eating.

2. Not once in my life have I ever craved a carrot stick.

3. I am not bouncy perky about giving up two of the greatest delights of my taste buds — Cheez-Its and box-mix brownies. In fact, I've even asked God if it would be such a terribly difficult thing to swap the molecular structure of Cheez-Its for carrot sticks. They're both already orange. And, really, how hard could that be for someone who's turned water into wine?

4. I wasn't sure I had any business writing a book like this. I'm a simple Jesus girl on a journey to finding deeper motivation than just a number on my scale for getting and staying healthy.

You see, I'm not writing this book to beat your taste buds into submission. I'm not writing this book because I have discovered the magic diet program to get you skinny by tomorrow. And I'm definitely not writing this book because I'm an expert.

I'm writing this book because I've struggled way too long with my food choices and my weight. And word on the street says most of my girlfriends fight this same draining battle day in and day out as well.

Which brings me to the fifth thing you should know about me:

5. I started this journey weighing 167 pounds.

To some, this is a horrifyingly high number. For me, it was a sign I needed to make changes. I was heading in a dangerous direction with my weight and my health. Again. I had been as high as almost 200 pounds after the birth of my first child. And now I was headed straight back to a place I thought I'd never be again. Maybe it was because I was knocking on the door of my fortieth birthday, or perhaps it was because I had exhausted my search for the miraculous overnight solution. I finally realized the weight was going to continue to go up unless I made changes.

But the thought of taking the plunge and signing up for another diet made me want to sit down and cry. And eat. And cry some more. Then eat some more. Well, you get the not-so-flattering picture.

To others, 167 is a dream weight. In my case, the number itself was not the issue. The issue was how I felt mentally, spiritually, and physically. It was time to be honest with myself.

I think we all get to a place sometimes in our lives when we have to give a brutally honest answer to the question, "How am I doing?" It's not really a conversation we have with a friend or family member. It's one of those middle-of-the-night contemplations when there's no one to fool. There's no glossing over the realities staring us in the face.

I knew certain things about myself needed to change but it was easier to make excuses than it was to tackle them head on. Rationalizations are so appealing. See if you relate to any of these:

I'm good in every other area.

I make so many sacrifices already.

I need treats as a comfort in this season of life; I'll deal with my issues later.

I just can't give this up.

The Bible doesn't specifically say this is wrong.

It's not really a problem. If I really wanted to make a change, I could; I just don't want to right now.

Oh, for heaven's sake, everyone has issues. So what if this is mine?

And on and on and on.

But excuses always got me nowhere fast, especially when it came to healthy eating. I suspect if you've picked up this book, the same laundry list of rationalization scripts have played out in your mind.

So, the cycle continues day after day, week after week, year after year. A whole lifetime could be spent making excuses, giving in, feeling guilty, resolving to do better, mentally beating myself up for not sticking to my resolve, feeling like a failure, and then resigning myself to the fact that things can't change.

And I don't want to spend a lifetime in this cycle.

I suspect you don't either.

So, before you put this book down and give in to the unhealthy cravings screaming inside your head, wait for just a second. Don't let go. You've already spent a few minutes headed in the right direction by picking up this book and reading this far.

It is easier to make excuses than changes.

The book you hold in your hands could be the missing companion you've needed with every healthy eating plan you tried and cried over. I believe it will help you find your "want to." In addition to helping you find the desire to conquer your unhealthy cravings, it also holds the key to something very significant for most of us women — spiritual malnutrition. We feel overweight physically but underweight spiritually. Tying these two things together is the first step on one of the most significant journeys you'll ever take with God.

It reminds me of a journey described in Matthew 19. A rich young man comes to see Jesus and explains that he is following all the rules but still feels something missing from his pursuit of God. "All of these [rules] I have kept," he says to Jesus. "What do I still lack?" (Matthew 19:20).

I doubt Mick Jagger got his inspiration from this story but the young man's desperate question sure does remind me of his wildly popular song, "I can't get no satisfaction ... no, no, no."

Unsatisfied.

Lacking.

Incomplete.

Hollow.

Shallow.

What do I still lack?

In other words, *How do I really get close to God?*

Such a vulnerable question. Such a relatable question.

Jesus responds, "If you want to be perfect [whole], go, sell your possessions and give to the poor, and you will have treasure in heaven. Then come, follow me" (Matthew 19:21).

The rich young man then goes away sad because he won't give up the one thing that consumes him. He is so full with his riches he can't see how undernourished his soul is. He's just like people today who refuse healthier breakfast options like egg whites and fruit so they can fill themselves up with candy-sprinkled, chocolate-frosted doughnuts. Even when their sugar high crashes and they complain of splitting headaches, they steadfastly refuse to consider giving up their doughnuts.

In my past, sugar-filled life, I might have had some personal experience once or twice that led me to think of that frail little analogy.

Anyhow.

It's at this point in the biblical story that most of us ordinary Jesus girls start thinking of all the rich people we know. "Well, I sure hope they get this message. Good thing I'm not rich. Good thing this doesn't apply to me. Good thing Jesus doesn't ask me to sacrifice in this way."

Or does He?

Jesus didn't mean this as a sweeping command for everyone who has a lot of money. Jesus meant this for any of us who wallow in whatever abundance we have. I imagine Jesus looked straight into this young man's soul and said, "I want you to give up the one thing you crave more than me. Then come, follow me."

Piercing thought, isn't it?

Suddenly, Jesus isn't just staring at the rich young man; He's also staring at me — the inside me. The part I can't cover up with excuses and makeup.

When Jesus says, "Follow me," it's not an invitation to drag our divided heart alongside us as we attempt to follow hard after God. When Jesus wants us to follow Him — really follow Him — it's serious business. Here's how Jesus describes it: "If anyone would come after me, he must deny himself and take up his cross and follow me" (Mark 8:34).

With Jesus, if we want to gain, we must give up.

If we want to be filled, we must deny ourselves.

If we want to truly get close to God, we'll have to distance ourselves from other things.

If we want to conquer our cravings, we'll have to redirect them to God.

God made us capable of craving so we'd have an unquenchable desire for more of Him, and Him alone. Nothing changes until we make the choice to redirect our misguided cravings to the only one capable of satisfying them.

Getting healthy isn't just about losing weight. It's not limited to adjusting our diet and hoping for good physical results. It's about recalibrating our souls so that we want to change — spiritually, physically, and mentally. And the battle really is in all three areas.

Spiritually. I had to ask God to give me the desire to be healthy. I knew a vanity-seeking "want to" would never last. Shallow desires produce only shallow efforts. I had to seek a spiritual "want to" empowered by God Himself.

So, I asked. I begged, actually. I cried out to God. And day by day, God gave me just enough "want to," laced with His strength, to be satisfied by healthy choices.

God also settled in my heart that this is an issue of great spiritual importance. Think of Eve and one of the first interactions recorded in the Bible between a woman and food. Obviously, the core of Eve's temptation was she wanted to be like God, knowing good and evil.

But we can't ignore the fact that *the serpent used food as a tool in the process.* If the very downfall of humanity was caused when Eve surrendered to a temptation to eat something she wasn't supposed to eat, I do think our struggles with food are important to God. We'll talk about this again later because there is a lot more to unpack where Eve's story is concerned. But I can honestly say that this is one of the most significant spiritual journeys I've ever dared to take with God. I hope you soon say the same thing.

Physically. The spiritual perspectives in this book may stir the soul, but the physical realities require turning those spiritual insights into practical choices.

When I began this journey, I finally had to admit the truth that what I eat matters. My weight is a direct reflection of my choices and the state of my health. I started with a visit to my doctor, which I highly encourage you to do before starting your healthy eating plan. The doctor ran several tests. At the time, I hoped he'd find something that was slightly off so I could miraculously lose all my extra weight as soon as he put me on medication. Alas, it wasn't to be. Except for some results that indicated I wasn't exercising regularly or making the healthiest food choices, the tests came back normal.

Hmfff. Why do doctors always say the same old thing about eating right and exercise? It's the standard doctor script for any issue I've ever had. Feeling sluggish? Eat better, move more. Feeling blue? Eat better, move more. I bet the next time I go in for a sore throat it will be the same thing. Eat better, move more. Have mercy. And we won't even go into the issues I have with the scale in my doctor's office. What is up with that thing? I am positive it weighs me heavy just to prove his point. *See? You need to eat better, move more.*

The doctor and the test results were right. My weight issues were directly linked to my food choices. Period. I had to admit it and do something about it.

Mentally. I had to decide I was tired of settling, tired of compromising. What happens when you delete "com" from the word *compromise*? You're left with a "promise." We were made for more than *compromise*. We were made for God's *promises* in every area of our lives.

Honestly, I am made for more than a vicious cycle of eating, gaining, stressing—eating, gaining, stressing ... I am made to rise up, do battle with my issues and, using the Lord's strength in me, defeat them—spiritually, physically, and mentally—to the glory of God.

Well, I hope you'll stick around on this journey of discovering your "want to." I can't promise it will be easy. But I can promise it will be the most empowering thing you've ever done. Just today I put on some jeans I never thought I'd wear again. And while my flesh did the happy dance of success, my soul was far from thoughts of vanity.

My soul felt free. I was amazed that I ever desired to satisfy my taste buds over satisfying my desire to break free from all the guilt, all the destruction, all the defeat.

Now I think it only fair to tell you one more fact. I still don't crave those blasted carrot sticks. I probably never will. But I found my "want to." I started eating better and moving more. I lost the weight. I feel great. And I have most certainly grown closer to God than ever before.

My truest cravings are satisfied—and yours can be too.

What's Really Going On Here?

Recently, a weight loss company came up with a brilliant advertising campaign. Maybe you've seen some of their ads. A little orange monster chases a woman around, tempting and taunting her with foods that obviously aren't a part of her healthy eating plan. The ads perfectly capture what it feels like to be harassed by cravings all day long.

While I've never seen this orange monster chasing me, I've felt its presence. My resolve feels strong until the next time I get hungry. And unhealthy choices are always so convenient. They are packaged and preserved and sing of salty and sugary highs tailor made for a hungry stomach. You don't find fresh fruits and veggies conveniently located in a nearby vending machine. So, I give in to that bag of chips or a candy bar because I am so hungry and it will only be for this time. These empty calories do nothing but taste good in the moment and then set me up for more unhealthy choices just a short time later.

We crave what we eat. So, the cycle continues day after day. Hunger pang after hunger pang. Craving after craving. The orange monster is there reminding me of all the delicious choices that would satisfy in ways healthy choices never would.

So, while the orange monster is a great way to visualize cravings, the ads fall short in their promise to really help a woman. The weight loss company's theory is to teach what foods are more filling and encourage consumption of those. But does that really help over-come cravings?

For me, it does not. The answer will never be found in only learn-ing to modify my choices. Choosing better foods is certainly a part of this journey. However, simply telling me to eat healthier foods that will help me feel full longer doesn't address the heart of the matter. I can feel full after a meal and still crave chocolate pie for dessert. Just feeling full isn't the answer to sticking with a healthy eating plan.

We crave what we eat.

If feeling full were the answer, then gastric bypass surgery should be 100 percent successful. This surgery shrinks the size of a person's stomach, thus shrinking the amount of food necessary to give them a full feeling. However, one study showed the failure rate for patients who were followed for at least ten years was 20.4 percent for mor-bidly obese patients and 34.9 percent for super obese patients.[1] Even a significant number of those whose lives are at stake — and who have drastic surgery to help them — can't always stop their cravings by simply feeling full.

So, what's really going on here?

I believe God made us to crave. Now before you think this is some sort of cruel joke by God, let me assure you that the object of our craving was never supposed to be food or other things people find themselves consumed by, such as sex or money or chasing after significance.

Think about the definition of the word _craving_. How would you define it? Dictionary.com defines _craving_ as something you long for, want greatly, desire eagerly, and beg for.[2] Now consider this expression of craving: "How lovely is your dwelling place, O LORD Almighty! My soul yearns, event faints, for the courts of the LORD; my heart and my flesh cry out for the living God" (Psalm 84:1 – 2).

Yes, we were made to crave — long for, want greatly, desire

eagerly, and beg for—God. Only God. But Satan wants to do everything possible to replace our craving for God with something else. Here's what the Bible says about this: "Do not love the world or anything in the world. If anyone loves the world, the love of the Father is not in him. For everything in the world—the cravings of sinful man, the lust of his eyes and the boasting of what he has and does—comes not from the Father but from the world" (1 John 2:15–16). The passage details three ways Satan tries to lure us away from loving God:

> *We were made to crave—long for, want greatly, desire eagerly, and beg for—God. Only God.*

- The cravings of the sinful man
- The lust of his eyes
- The boasting of what he has or does

Let's define these things. According to the commentary in my Life Application Study Bible (NIV), the cravings of the sinful man are misplaced physical desires—issues with our food or sex outside of marriage. In other words trying to get our physical needs met outside the will of God. The lust of the eyes is being enamored by material things. The New Living Translation actually equates the lust of the eyes as "a craving for everything we see." And lastly, the boasting of what one has or does describes the actions of someone chasing what she thinks will make her feel significant.

> *Cravings* = trying to get our physical desires met outside the will of God
>
> *Lust of eyes* = trying to get our material desires met outside the will of God
>
> *Boasting* = trying to get our need for significance met outside the will of God

Remember in the introduction when we briefly talked about

Eve? She was lured by the serpent into eating the forbidden fruit. As I was studying this story I realized how intentionally Satan chooses his tactics. He knows where we are weak. He desires to lure us away from God. And he knows what works ... the cravings of the sinful man, the lust of his eyes, and the boasting of what he has or does.

Satan used all three tactics with Eve. "When the woman saw that the fruit of the tree was good for food [cravings of the sinful man] and pleasing to the eye [lust of the eyes], and also desirable for gaining wisdom [boasting of what she has or does], she took some and ate it" (Genesis 3:6). Eve was tempted in precisely the same three ways the 1 John passage warns us not to be lured away from loving God.

But it doesn't stop there. Look at how Jesus was tempted:

> Then Jesus was led by the Spirit into the desert to be tempted by the devil. After fasting forty days and forty nights, he was hungry. The tempter came to him and said, "If you are the Son of God, tell these stones to become bread."
>
> Jesus answered, "It is written: 'Man does not live on bread alone, but on every word that comes from the mouth of God.' "
>
> Then the devil took him to the holy city and had him stand on the highest point of the temple. "If you are the Son of God," he said, "throw yourself down. For it is written: 'He will command his angels concerning you, and they will lift you up in their hands, so that you will not strike your foot against a stone.' "
>
> Jesus answered him, "It is also written: 'Do not put the Lord your God to the test.' "
>
> Again, the devil took him to a very high mountain and showed him all the kingdoms of the world and their splendor. "All this I will give you," he said, "if you will bow down and worship me."
>
> Jesus said to him, "Away from me, Satan! For it is written: 'Worship the Lord your God, and serve him only.' "

Then the devil left him, and angels came and attended him.
(Matthew 4:1 – 11)

Again, the pattern of temptation is the same:

Cravings: Satan appealed to Jesus' physical cravings for food.

Lust of the eyes: The devil promised Jesus entire kingdoms if He
would bow down to the god of materialism.

Boasting: The enemy enticed Jesus to prove His significance by
forcing God to command angels to save Him.

But here's the significant difference between Eve and Jesus. Eve
was saturated in the object of her desire. Jesus was saturated in
God's truth.

I obviously wasn't in the garden with Eve, but based on three
phrases from Genesis 3:6, I can only infer she never took her eyes
off the fruit as she: *saw that the food was good, pleasing to the eye,
and desirable.* She didn't walk away and give herself time to really
consider her choice. She didn't consult Adam. She didn't consider
the truth of what God had clearly instructed. She didn't talk to God.
She focused only on the object of her obsession.

Remember what I said at the beginning of this chapter … we
crave what we eat. If I make healthy choices over a period of time,
it seems to reprogram my taste buds. The more veggies and fruit I
eat, the more veggies and fruit I crave. However, if I eat brownies
and chips, I crave brownies and chips in the worst kind of way. Eve
craved what she focused on. We consume what we think about. And
what we think about can consume us if we're not careful.

Jesus sets a beautiful example of breaking this vicious cycle of
being consumed by cravings. It's even more powerful when we
understand that Jesus, unlike Eve, was in a completely deprived
state. Eve was in a garden of paradise with her every need provided
for. Jesus had been in a desert, fasting for forty days. I can't imagine

a more deprived state. And yet, He held strong and set a powerful example of how to escape the vicious grip of temptation. He quoted God's Word. And so can we. When we feel deprived and frustrated and consumed with wanting unhealthy choices, we too can rely on God's Word to help us.

With each temptation, Jesus, without hesitation, quoted Scripture that refuted Satan's temptation. Truth is powerful. The more saturated we are with truth, the more powerful we'll be in resisting our temptations. And the more we'll naturally direct our cravings where they should be directed — to the Author of all truth.

Cravings. Are they a curse or a blessing? The answer to that depends on what we're craving. And what we're craving will always depend on whatever we're consuming ... the object of our desire or God and His truth.

Truth is powerful. The more saturated we are with truth, the more powerful we'll be in resisting our temptations.

In the next chapter we'll talk about how to practically consume God's truth in a way that truly satisfies. For now, consider what it means to the success of your journey to quote Scripture in the midst of a craving attack. One of the most meaningful Scriptures I used in this process is " 'Everything is permissible' — but not everything is beneficial" (1 Corinthians 10:23). We'll talk about this Scripture more in a later chapter, but I quoted it over and over to remind myself that I could have that brownie or those chips, but they wouldn't benefit me in any way. That thought empowered me to make a beneficial choice rather than wallowing in being deprived of an unhealthy choice. For other helpful Scriptures, check out the section starting on page 195. Make a point to write out meaningful verses for this journey and quote them aloud each time the orange monster tries to talk you into tarrying with him a while.

I know it's a battle, sister. But we aren't rendered powerless. The more saturated we are with God's truth, the more powerfully resistant we become. Stick with me here — this isn't a plastic Christian answer. It's one that will change our lives if we let it.

Personal Reflections

1. One weight loss company personifies craving as a little orange monster that chases us around, tempting us to eat unhealthy foods. Take a moment to reflect on your own experience of craving, recently and over time.

   • If you could personify craving based on your experience of it, what form might it take? Would it be like the little orange monster or would it take a different shape? Describe what your craving looks like and how it behaves.

   • If you could sit down and have a conversation with this imaginary craving, what do you think it might say to you? What questions would you want to ask it? How do you imagine it might respond?

2. How do you respond to the idea that God made us to crave (page 20)? Have you ever pursued a craving — a longing, passion, or desire — that made a positive contribution to your life? What do you think distinguishes that kind of craving from the craving that leads you to eat in unhealthy ways?

3. If it's true that we are made to crave, how might it change the way you understand your cravings? Do you believe there could be any benefits to listening to your cravings rather than trying to silence them? If so, what might those benefits be? If not, why not?

4. The Bible describes three ways Satan tries to lure us away from loving God: cravings, lust of the eyes, and boasting (1 John 2:15 – 16). Lysa explains how Satan used these tactics with both

Eve and Jesus (pages 22–23). Using the list below, think back over the last twenty-four hours or the last few days to see if you recognize how you may have been tempted in similar ways.

• *Cravings: meeting physical desires outside the will of God.* In what ways were you tempted by desires for things such as food, alcohol, drugs, or sex?

• *Lust of the eyes: meeting material desires outside the will of God.* In what ways were you tempted by desires for material things — clothing, financial portfolio, appliances, vacation plans, cosmetics, home décor, electronics, etc.?

• *Boasting: meeting needs for significance outside the will of God.* In what ways were you tempted by desires to prop up your significance — perhaps by name dropping, exaggerating, feigning humility or other virtues, doing something just because you knew it would been observed by others, etc.?

Of the three kinds of temptations, which is the most difficult for you to resist? Which is the easiest to resist? Why?

5. Jesus quotes the truth of Scripture to defeat temptation (page 22). Have you ever used Scripture in this way? What was the result? How do you feel about the idea of using this approach to address your unhealthy eating patterns?

2

Replacing My Cravings

I roll over and look at the clock. Another day. Beyond all reason and rationality, I slide out of bed and strip off everything that might weigh even the slightest ounce as I head to the scale. Maybe today will be the day the scale will be my friend and not reveal my secrets. Maybe somehow overnight the molecular structure of my body shifted and today I will magically weigh less.

But no. I yank out my ponytail holder — hey, it's gotta weigh something — and decide to try again. But the scale doesn't change its mind the second time. It is not my friend this day.

Vowing to do better, eat healthier, and make good choices, I head to the kitchen only to have my resolve melt like the icing on the cinnamon rolls my daughter just pulled from the oven. Yum. Oh, who cares what the scale says when this roll speaks such love and deliciousness.

Two and a half cinnamon rolls later, I decide tomorrow will be a much better day to keep my promises to eat healthier. And since this is my last day to eat what I want, I better live it up. Another cinnamon roll, please.

The next morning I roll over and look at the clock. Another day. Beyond all reason and rationality, I slide out of bed and strip off everything that might weigh even the slightest ounce as I head to the scale. Maybe today will be the day. But once again it isn't. I yank out my ponytail holder and try again. But no.

Vowing to do better, eat healthier, and make good choices, I head into my day only to find myself making more excuses, rationalizations, and promises for later.

Always later.

And the cycle I've come to hate and feel powerless to stop continues. Who could I talk to about this? If I admit my struggle with food to my friends, they might try to hold me accountable the next time we go out. And what if I'm not in the mood to be questioned about my nachos con queso with extra sour cream?

I'll just tell them I'll be starting on Monday, and they'll be fine with it. They don't think I need to make changes.

But I did need to make changes. I knew it. Because this wasn't really about the scale or what clothing size I was; it was about this battle that raged in my heart. I thought about, craved, and arranged my life too much around food. So much so, I knew it was something that God was challenging me to surrender to His control. Really surrender. Surrender to the point where I'd make radical changes for the sake of my spiritual health perhaps even more than my physical health.

This wasn't really about the scale or what clothing size I was; it was about this battle that raged in my heart.

Part of my surrender was asking myself a really raw question.

May I ask you this same raw question?

Is it possible we love and rely on food more than we love and rely on God?

Now, before you throw this book across the room and curse my existence, hear me out. This question is crucial. I had to see the purpose of my struggle as something more than wearing smaller sizes and getting compliments from others. These things would be nice but not as appealing in the moment as that cinnamon roll or those chips or that brownie.

It had to be about something more than just me.

I had to get honest enough to admit it: I relied on food more than I relied on God. I craved food more than I craved God. Food was my comfort. Food was my reward. Food was my joy. Food was what I turned to in times of stress, sadness, and even in times of happiness.

And I hated admitting that. I felt stupid admitting that. I felt like such a spiritual failure.

I told a couple of people about it and most seemed supportive. But one well-meaning lady quipped what others would echo in the months that followed, "You're making this diet thing a spiritual journey? Does God really care about our food?"

Yes, I think He does. As I scan the list of Scriptures found at the end of this book, I do think it's an issue God takes seriously. As a matter of fact, I think it is an issue that deserves to be studied with the desire to excavate the many truths the Bible has for those struggling with unhealthy cravings.

God never intended for us to want anything more than we want Him. Just the slightest glimpse into His Word proves that. Look at what the Bible says about God's chosen people, the Israelites, when they wanted food more than they wanted God: "They willfully put God to the test by demanding the food they craved" (Psalm 78:18). Yikes.

And what became of them? They never reached the Promised Land. These people wandered in the desert for forty years and no one but Joshua and Caleb was allowed to enter the land flowing with milk and honey. Not one. God waited until every one from that generation died before He allowed Joshua and Caleb to lead the younger generation into the abundant life they desired with all their heart.

I don't know about you, but I don't want to wander about in a "desert," unable to enter into the abundant life God has for me because I willfully put Him to the test over food!

When I started, I knew this battle would be hard—harder than I ever imagined. But through it all I determined to make God, rather than food, my focus. Each time I craved something I knew wasn't part of my plan, I used that craving as a prompt to pray. I craved a lot. So, I found myself praying a lot.

Don't rush past that last paragraph. I used my cravings for food as a prompting to pray. It was my way of tearing down the tower of impossibility before me and building something new. My tower of impossibility was food. Brick by brick, I imagined myself dismantling the food tower and using those same bricks to build a walkway of prayer, paving the way to victory.

Each time I craved something I knew wasn't part of my plan, I used that craving as a prompt to pray. I craved a lot. So, I found myself praying a lot.

Did this simple visualization make it easier? Sometimes it did. And other times my cravings for unhealthy food made me cry. Seriously, cry. Sometimes I wound up on the floor in my closet, praying with tears running down my face. And I gave myself permission to cry, just like the psalmist: "Give ear to my words, O LORD, consider my sighing. Listen to my cry for help, my King and my God, for to you I pray. In the morning, O LORD, you hear my voice; in the morning I lay my requests before you and wait in expectation" (Psalm 5:1–3). And that is literally what I did. Each and every craving became another brick I could lay on my walkway of prayer.

"God, I want a biscuit this morning. Instead, I'm eating poached eggs. I'm thankful for these eggs but I'll be honest in saying my cravings for other things are hard to resist. But, instead of wallowing in what I *can't* have, I'm making the choice to celebrate what I *can* have."

"God, it's 10:00 a.m. and I'm craving again. I want those snack crackers that are literally screaming my name. But instead of reaching for those crackers, I'm praying. I'll be honest, I don't want to pray. I want those crackers. But, instead, I'm going to have a handful of almonds and brick by brick … prayer by prayer … lay a path for victory."

"God, it's lunchtime and all my friends are heading out for Mexican. I love Mexican. I could seriously justify myself right into a big bowl of chips and guacamole right now. It's been a tough day. But once again I'm choosing to pray instead of getting stuck in my craving. Help me, God, to feel satisfied with healthier choices."

And that's how my prayers continued throughout the day. Laying my requests before God and, like the psalmist says, waiting in expectation (Psalm 5:3).

Then, one morning it finally happened. I got up and for the first time in a long while, I felt incredibly empowered. I still did the same crazy routine with the scale — no clothes, no ponytail holder — but I only stepped on it once. The numbers hadn't changed yet, but my heart had. One day of victory tasted better than any of that food I'd given up ever could. I had waited in expectation using prayer as my guide and I did it.

I did it that day and the next. Then the next. Why not shoot for four victorious days in a row? And then maybe one more.

I can't promise you there won't be any more tears. There will. And I can't promise the scale magically drops as quickly as you wish it would. It probably won't. But it will be a start. A really good start.

Personal Reflections

1. Lysa describes her morning ritual with the scale and her failed efforts to eat healthier as a vicious cycle she felt powerless to stop (page 28). When it comes to your relationship with food, what repeated behaviors or events describe the cycle you experience and feel powerless to stop?

2. There are many reasons we have for wanting to eat differently —losing weight, fitting into a favorite pair of jeans, looking good for an important event. What reasons motivate your desire to eat healthier? Do these reasons give your struggles with food a purpose strong enough to help you resist unhealthy eating? How do you respond to Lysa's statement, "I had to see the purpose of my struggle as something more than wearing smaller sizes and getting compliments from others.... It had to be about something more than just me"?

3. "I had to get honest enough to admit it: I relied on food more than I relied on God. I craved food more than I craved God. Food was my comfort. Food was my reward. Food was my joy. Food was what I turned to in times of stress, sadness, and even in times of happiness" (page 29). Consider your eating experiences over the last few days or weeks. Using the list below, can you recall specific situations in which you turned to food for these reasons?

   • Comfort

   • Reward

   • Joy

   • Stress

   • Sadness

   • Happiness

Keeping the same situations in mind, how do you imagine your experiences might have been different if you had relied on God, craved God, instead of turning to food?

4. How do you respond to the idea of using your cravings as a prompt to pray? How has prayer helped or failed to help in your previous food battles?

5. Brick by brick (or craving by craving), Lysa dismantled her tower of impossibility and used the same bricks to build a walkway of prayer, paving the path to victory. Brick by brick is an effective way to dismantle something but it also takes time and careful work. In your battles with food, are you more likely to choose a drastic, quick-fix approach or a moderate but longer-term approach? What thoughts or feelings emerge when you consider dismantling your own tower of impossibility one craving at a time?

Getting a Plan

L ast spring I took a shortcut through a neighborhood and caught a glimpse of a man planting a flower garden. It was just a quick glance, but long enough to produce a lingering thought: *I wish I had a pretty garden.*

For years I've looked at other people's flowers and secretly wished for my own lush display. However, the glimpse of this man with his hands digging deep into the earth brought a new revelation. He has a garden because he invests time and energy to make it. He didn't wish it into being. He didn't hope it into being. He didn't just wake up one day and find that a garden of glorious blooms had miraculously popped up from the dirt.

No.

He worked at it. He sacrificed for it.

Day after day. Row by row. Seed by seed. Plant by plant. It took effort, intentionality, sweat equity, and determination. Then it took time and commitment before he ever saw any fruit from his labor.

But eventually, there was a bloom ... and then another ... and then another. I saw this man's flowers and wished for my own—without a clue about all the work that had gone into producing them. I want the flowers but not the work. Isn't that the way it is with many things in life—we want the results but have no desire to put in the work required?

Besides a garden, I also wished for a thinner body for years but was lax about actually changing what I ate. When it came to eating, I excused away the necessary discipline. Then I'd catch myself wishing I were thinner and making excuses about my age and metabolism, lamenting the unfairness of my genetic disposition and blah, blah, blah.

The reality is, I can't eat like an athletic teenager and then complain about my extra layers of fluff.

Or my pants size.

Or my tummy pooch.

Or my arms that are starting to wave back at me when I raise them.

I can't wish blooms into place any more than I can wish fat away. It's just the cold, hard reality.

But I knew I needed a plan.

I can't eat like an athletic teenager and then complain about my extra layers of fluff.

I had a friend who'd found a nutritionist she really liked. She followed a plan, got her issues under control, lost weight, kept it off, and experienced the empowering feeling of success. As she was telling me about her plan, she looked across the table and said, "Lysa, if you do this, it will work."

I wanted to believe her. I desperately wanted to believe her. I knew I'd be making an appointment with this same nutritionist.

The day of my first appointment, I sat in my car and chuckled at my choice for a *last meal*—the meal before I'd have to make changes.

I stared down at the paper plate. Minutes before, it had been piled high with slices of Chef Boyardee pizza. Cheap, boxed pizza had been the absolute delight of my childhood taste buds. Who am I kidding? It had been the absolute delight of my adulthood as well. And if my food choice alone didn't seal the deal that changes needed to be made, my next move certainly did.

I licked the plate. I did. Yes, I did. If this would be the last time I'd enjoy this delicacy, I was for sure not leaving a drop of sauce on the plate. Not a drop.

Then I checked the rearview mirror for any stray evidence. Getting on a scale in front of another woman would be horrible enough. I didn't want to compound this mortifying situation with her telling me I had pizza sauce smeared across my cheek. Cheap pizza sauce at that.

I looked myself straight in the rearview mirror and, with nothing but grit and determination, ignored the screams of my taste buds and stepped out of the car. After tucking my muffin top into the waist of my jeans, my body nodded in agreement with my head: this is something we must do. My taste buds never did agree with the rest of my body that day.

Inside the nutritionist's office, I was told I was overweight. This was not news to me. I had gone up two pants sizes over the past year and now even my big pants were protesting. And not even my trick of standing on the bathroom scale with only one foot—and no ponytail holder—could diminish the escalating numbers.

Something had to give.

Someone had to learn the discipline of giving up some things and that someone was me. And those "things" were poor food choices that were sabotaging my body, my mental energy, and even my spirit.

Food had become like a drug. And honestly, it's a good drug choice for a Christian woman. Every church event I attended readily provided my drug out in the open with no hesitation or judgment.

Poor food choices were sabotaging my body, my mental energy, and even my spirit. Food had become like a drug.

I didn't struggle with the addictions most people refer to when they find out someone has issues with food. I was not anorexic or bulimic. I never binged and purged. I wasn't overeating until I made myself sick or anything like that.

I was just eating too much of the wrong kinds of foods and felt trapped in a cycle of hunger. I felt hungry all the time. And I felt discouraged and down about my escalating weight yet powerless to make the necessary changes.

I had lost weight before, but I couldn't keep it off for any extended time. My changes were always temporary; therefore my results were also temporary. I was too dependent on food for comfort and saw no need for a long-term discipline plan for my eating. I wanted to eat what I wanted, when I wanted, in the quantities I wanted. So, despite exercising, my food choices caught up with me and my changing body revealed all my secrets.

That's both the blessing and the curse of issues with food. Poor choices with food will rat me out every time—if not in my waistline, then in my energy level and my overall well-being.

I left the nutritionist's office that day with a plan. Under her supervision and with a weekly weigh-in to hold me accountable, I felt empowered for the first time in a long while.

The plan I chose was strict and restrictive. I knew in my heart it had to be. I had to break the addictive cycles my taste buds had grown to crave. I needed to train my body to not be hungry all the time. I had to keep my blood sugar in check.

The healthy eating plan I adopted then and maintain now is a balanced protein-carbohydrate plan. I learned correct portion sizes, food combining, when to eat and what to eat. I still eat carbohydrates, but I'm limited in how much and what kind. I don't eat most breads, potatoes, rice, corn, pasta, or other starchy things. Mainly, I eat low-fat meats, veggies, and fruits.

Wait! Wait! I'm not saying this has to be your plan. (You need to do your research, consult your doctor, and create a healthy and realistic plan for *your* everyday life.) I'm saying this is *my* plan and,

believe it or not, I've grown to love it. Notice I said "*grown* to love it."
I won't deny there have been some really hard days.

My plan is realistic for me because the foods I eat are things I can
buy at my local grocery store and because my family can eat what I
eat for the most part. However, they usually have starches that I skip.

This journey will require you to make some tough sacrifices, but
I've come to look at this process as embracing healthy choices rather
than denying myself. There are lessons to be learned and perspectives to be gained in the season of embracing healthy choices. These
will not just be physical lessons. The mental
and spiritual lessons gained in this time will
be the very thing that will equip you for the
long haul. And keep you healthy and blos-
soming just like that man's garden.

Speaking of gardens, I have a funny
truth to share about the healthy eating plan I
chose. Basically, I eat what a wild animal eats
—meat and things that grow naturally from
the earth. Only I cook my food and use man-
ners. I was immediately encouraged by the
possibilities of this new eating plan because
I have yet to see an overweight animal in the wild lamenting over
excess cellulite.

This journey will require you to make some tough sacrifices, but I've come to look at this process as embracing healthy choices rather than denying myself.

Think about it.

And while you are thinking that silly little thought, think about
and pray for some friends to join you on this journey. I have to tell
you, having friends to walk through the same healthy eating plan as
me has been such a help. Getting a plan is the first crucial step; getting a friend or two to join you is the next.

But, in the meantime, don't be expecting any fresh cut flowers
from my garden. That is still but a wish.

A girl can't do it all, you know.

Personal Reflections

1. What thoughts, images, or emotions do you associate with the word *plan*? Are you the kind of person who says, "I love it when a plan comes together!" or are you more likely to say, "Plan-schman, can't we all just go with the flow?"

2. Are there areas of your life in which having a plan works well for you? For example, in your finances, for vacation trips, accomplishing daily tasks, reaching professional goals, reading through the Bible in a year. In these areas of your life, does having a plan feel empowering or restrictive? Do your feelings change when the plan is about food, what you will eat and not eat?

3. "My changing body revealed all my secrets. . . . Poor choices with food will rat me out every time" (page 38). What is the relationship between food and secrets? What secrets do you think your body reveals?

4. Choosing a healthy eating plan that works for you may require research, experimentation, and consultation with your doctor or other health care professionals. How does the prospect of doing these things make you feel? Does it energize you and help you to feel equipped or does it overwhelm you and make you feel discouraged?

5. Lysa described her food plan but emphasized the importance of choosing a healthy plan that works for you. What words or phrases would you use to describe the kind of plan you think would be realistic for you over the long term? On a scale of one to ten, how hopeful are you that you can find a realistic food plan, one that you can grow to love just as Lysa grew to love her food plan?

Friends Don't Let Friends Eat before Thinking

*S*top, *in the name of love, before you break my heart. Think it over.* Who would have ever thought this classic tune by the Supremes could apply to so much more than a girlfriend warning her wayward beau. This song was the soundtrack to many of my silly-little-girl dance fests. But contained within the singsong melody is a very powerful statement, "Think it over."

I wonder how many bad choices and severe consequences could have been averted if that three-word statement had been applied.

Sometimes, we can muster up the gumption to *think it over* on our own and redirect our steps away from the slippery slope of compromise. But, more times than not, we need measures of accountability.

For me, one of the most effective accountability measures has been mutually tracking progress with friends. I have one friend, Marybeth, who started ahead of me and who has been an invaluable source of encouragement and perspective. She's the one I mentioned earlier who leaned across the table and said, "If you do this healthy eating plan, it will work." I clung to that statement when I had a little breakdown.

> *For me, one of the most effective accountability measures has been mutually tracking progress with friends.*

The first three weeks of my new eating plan, things went well. I only struggled with being hungry the first ten days. Things were smooth sailing until the start of week four. At that point, I think my body went through sugar withdrawals. I'm not kidding.

All of my systems were out of whack. I felt like I had the flu one day, severe allergies the next, and then stomach issues for a week after that. I might have thought I had some kind of terrible sickness, except I didn't. It was definitely my angry little self demanding I give my body some SUGAR NOW!

I felt awful. I could hardly exercise. I had to nap—and if you know me in real life you know what a shocker that is! Part of me was seriously ready to throw in the towel, head to the boxed brownie aisle of the grocery store, and ask if anyone knew how to hook up an IV line between me and Betty Crocker.

We must be aware that desperation breeds degradation. In other words, when what is lacking in life goes from being an annoyance to an anxiety we run the risk of compromising in ways we never thought we would.

I find it interesting that a verse many of us know and quote— how the devil prowls about like a roaring lion looking for someone to devour—is tucked right at the end of a passage that says, "Cast all your anxiety on him because he cares for you. Be self-controlled and alert" (1 Peter 5:7 – 8).

You see, when we determine to get healthy, we will have to give up certain things and change our habits. Doing this can make us feel anxious. That's why we must have friends to help us remember that what we're giving up in the short term will help us get what we really want in the long term. If we forget to be self-controlled and alert, we are prime targets for Satan to usher us right away from the new standards we've set in our life. That's degradation.

Yes, desperation breeds degradation.

A person who thinks she would never steal gets into a financial bind and suddenly finds herself skimming money from the register at work.

A person who thinks she'd never have sex before marriage feels physically pressured by someone she desperately wants love from and suddenly finds herself in bed with him.

A person committed to getting healthy forgets to pack her healthy snacks and suddenly feels it's urgent to zip by the vending machine and grab some chips and a candy bar just this one time.

> *Friends help us remember that what we're giving up in the short term will help us get what we really want in the long term.*

Be aware and be on guard, sweet sister. Know that these are devised schemes to lure you away from your commitments. Find a friend who can speak rationality into your irrational impulses. A friend who will hold you accountable, speak the truth in love, and pray for you.

Look at a great example of how desperation breeds degradation in the Old Testament story of Esau. Esau was the older of two twins, a skillful hunter, while the younger twin, Jacob, was more of a homebody. The Scriptures say:

> Once when Jacob was cooking some stew, Esau came in from the open country, famished. He said to Jacob, "Quick, let me have some of that red stew! I'm famished!" (That is why he was also called Edom.)
>
> Jacob replied, "First sell me your birthright."
>
> "Look, I am about to die," Esau said. "What good is the birthright to me?"
>
> But Jacob said, "Swear to me first." So he swore an oath to him, selling his birthright to Jacob.
>
> Then Jacob gave Esau some bread and some lentil stew. He ate and drank, and then got up and left.
>
> So Esau despised his birthright. (Genesis 25:29–34)

The thing that strikes me about this story is how much Esau gave up for just a few moments of physical satisfaction. He sacrificed what was good in the long term for what felt good in the short term. He gave up who he was in a moment of desperation.

Had a true friend of Esau's heard this interaction with Jacob, surely he would have spoken some rationality into Esau's irrational impulses.

That's what Marybeth was for me—a voice of reason, stability, and rationality. While she held fast with her assurances, I cried. Cried *tears*, y'all—big tears over the lack of sugar and salty treats and the feelings of temporary highs they always delighted in giving me. After calling her, I'd lie down on my bathroom floor and beg God for His help. To say I was miserable was an understatement. But the thought of Marybeth asking me if I had persevered and not being able to say yes was unimaginable. If she could press through her withdrawal days, so could I.

Then the day after my worst day, all my symptoms vanished. Suddenly I felt great. My body was strong, my emotions were in check, my energy level was sky high.

Just like Marybeth said would happen. Amazing. Persevering through my breakdown ushered me into a sweet place of breakthrough and suddenly I started seeing tangible results. It felt so good to not dread getting dressed in the morning. It was a major perk in life to wear clothes that actually fit. Now, granted, at this point, they were still my "big clothes" but being able to put them on with comfort and ease was a great step in the right direction.

It also was crucial to have the accountability of another friend, Holly, who started this healthy eating plan at the same time I did. We both knew it would be hard, so we committed to praying for one another as well as holding each other accountable. Each day we talked about what we'd be eating that day. Every week we reported our weight to one another. We talked through each struggle, each temptation that seemed so consuming, each step both good and bad.

Knowing I couldn't hide little cheats here and there from Holly kept me from slipping. I couldn't stand the thought of having to tell her I'd messed up — so I didn't. Our motto became, "If it's not part of our plan, we don't put it in our mouths."

If you don't have a friend who is willing to take this journey with you by changing her eating habits, don't be discouraged. Find a friend who is willing to take the journey with you in prayer. Be honest with her about your struggles and ask her to commit to praying fervently for you and with you.

Honestly, I NEVER EVER thought I could really give up eating bread, pasta, rice, potatoes, and sugar. I didn't think I could go a day without those staples of my daily eating patterns. No way.

But seeing the success of Marybeth ahead of me and having Holly willing to sacrifice with me gave my brain permission to stop — in the name of love — and think it over.

While you'll have to find a friend to either do a healthy eating plan with you or one who will pray you through it, let me be the friend that has journeyed ahead of you. Let me be that voice that reaches across your doubts to say, "If you follow the healthy eating plan you've chosen, it will work and it most certainly will be worth it." And when you get into possible trouble with temptation, remember to "stop in the name of love." Let your love for your friends, who are standing with you, and your love for the Lord, who wants you to honor Him in the way you treat your body, make you think it over.

Thinking it over and knowing I'd have to admit a slip to my friend has helped me walk away from countless bowls of chips and platters of brownies. The temporary pleasure of one brownie would never be worth me having to tell my accountability partners that I made the choice to mess up. That I made the choice to go back on my commitment … our commitment. That I made the choice to go back to my brokenness and set back all that I've attained. That's a high price for a brownie. Yes, accountability is crucial.

Now, I know if I would have been reading this just a few years ago, I would be rolling my eyes right now and saying, "Whatever! Accountability is not something I need with food, for heaven's sake." But the vast majority of us respond very well to accountability in other areas of life. Consider these scenarios:

- When you see a policeman checking the speed of passing cars, are you more likely to go the speed limit?
- When you have a meeting with your boss first thing the next morning, are you more likely to be on time?
- If you know you will be called upon to share your answers in Bible study, are you more likely to do your lesson?
- If you are having friends over for dinner, are you more likely to tidy your house?
- When your bank account is low on funds, are you more likely to slow down your spending?

If you answered yes to at least three of these five questions, you are someone who responds well to accountability. In most of these cases, we stop and we think it over — maybe not in the name of love, but definitely in the name of accountability.

So, are you ready? Take time to prayerfully consider the right healthy eating plan for you. Talk to your friends to see who might be willing to join you. And then start walking toward the healthy life that is possible for you.

Personal Reflections

1. When a friend experiences success with healthy food choices and losing weight, do you feel encouraged and inspired by her example, or do you feel discouraged and envious? Do you communicate your feelings to your friend or keep them to yourself?

2. Complete this sentence: I do/do not want to invite a friend to help me on my journey to healthy eating because _____ _____.

3. If accountability is crucial, what is the biggest challenge you face in making accountability part of your healthy eating plan?

4. If you were to imagine a life-giving experience of accountability, one that empowers you and helps you to feel companioned rather than alone in your struggles, how would you describe that experience? What kind of person would you want to be accountable to? What do you hope this person would do for you? What do you hope they would *not* do? How would you determine whether or not the relationship is providing effective accountability?

Made for More

There typically is a honeymoon phase at the start of a new healthy eating plan and nothing tempts you away from healthy choices. But then you're invited to a party. Your friends are quick to say, "Oh come on, just one won't hurt. This is a special day." And that cheesecake does look good. The tortilla chips and salsa are irresistible. It is a special night. You can just start again tomorrow. Or this weekend. Or Monday. Or the first of next month.

It is so tempting to give in. Set things in reverse. Pretend it won't matter.

But it does matter and not just for the physical or mental setback. It's the denial of a fundamental spiritual truth that will make a healthy eating plan fall apart time and time again. What is this truth? *We were made for more than this.* More than this failure, more than this cycle, more than being ruled by taste buds. We were made for victory. Sometimes we just have to find our way to that truth.

We were made for victory. Sometimes we just have to find our way to that truth.

When I was a senior in high school I was invited to a college party. I had a friend who'd graduated the year before me and became my favorite person in the world the day she invited me to her sorority party.

Cool doesn't even begin to describe what I felt as me and my pink jelly shoes made our way into that party. By the end of the night we were giggling over the attention given to us by two good-looking college boys. As the party died down, they invited us over to their place.

Part of me was so flattered, I wanted to go. A much bigger part of me didn't. But plans got made and before I knew it we were getting into their car and driving away.

I was not a Christian at this point in my life. Not even close. And I certainly can't say I'd ever heard God speak to me, but in the midst of this situation, I did.

"This isn't you, Lysa. You were made for more than this."

Truth. A gift of truth. Planted deep within me when God personally knit me together. Untied and presented at just the right time.

I wound up making an excuse for a quick exit and walked back to my car alone that night. I mentally beat myself up for acting like a young, immature high schooler who couldn't handle being a college party girl. But looking back, I want to stand up on a chair and clap, clap, clap for my little high schooler self!

There were other seasons of my growing-up years when I heard this truth loud and clear within the confines of my soul and, sadly, I refused to listen. These were the darkest years of my life. I wasn't made to live a life that dishonors the Lord.

None of us are.

"You were made for more, Lysa, you were made for more." I remembered it especially in those early weeks of my new healthy eating adventure when I was tempted by one million assaults on my sugar-deprived taste buds. I just kept mentally repeating . . . *made for more . . . made for more.*

And though my quest pales in comparison to the importance of a high schooler trying to keep her purity, hunger is hunger. Temptation is temptation. Desire is desire. So, maybe they aren't so different after all.

Each time I remember this truth, I am challenged and invigorated by it all over again. We were made for more.

What a great truth for us all. What a great truth to use while rewriting the "go-to" scripts that play in our head every time we're tempted. Rewriting the go-to scripts is one of the most crucial steps toward permanent progress. Remember the "scripts" I mentioned at the beginning of this chapter and earlier in this book? The excuses? The rationalizations? The "I'll do better tomorrow" escape clauses?

We have to rewrite those by getting into the habit of saying other things. And the first of these is, "I was made for more." Wrapped in this truth is a wisdom and revelation that unlocks great power available to all Christians.

And isn't power what girls in pursuit of making healthy life changes really need? We need a power beyond our frail attempts and fragile resolve. A power greater than our taste buds, hormones, temptations, and our inborn female demand for chocolate. Yes, the truth of who we are and the power to live out that truth—that's what we need.

Read what the apostle Paul writes about this amazing power available to us "made for more" girls, and note the emphasized phrases, which we'll take a closer look at in a moment:

> *I keep asking* that the God of our Lord Jesus Christ, the *glorious Father,* may give you the Spirit of wisdom and revelation, *so that you may know him better.* I pray also that the eyes of your heart may be enlightened in order that you may know the hope to which he has called you, the riches of his glorious inheritance in the saints, and *his incomparably great power for us* who believe." (Ephesians 1:17–19, emphasis added)

Now I realize it is hard to take a passage like this, hold it up to a decadent piece of chocolate cake, and instantly feel the power to walk away. But if we unpack this passage, understand its richness, and then practice its truth, it's amazing how empowered we'll be. So, let's take a closer look at some key words and phrases.

Be Persistent:
"I Keep Asking"

"I keep asking." We must ask God to join us in this journey. And this won't be a one-time exercise. Paul doesn't ask for wisdom one time. Paul asks over and over and over again. So should we. We need to ask for God's wisdom, revelation, and intervening power to be an integral part of our food choices from now on.

Why not make this a daily prayer, first thing in the morning, before we've eaten a thing that day: "God, I recognize I am made for more than the vicious cycle of being ruled by food. I need to eat to live, not live to eat. So, I keep asking for Your wisdom to know what to eat and Your indwelling power to walk away from things that are not beneficial for me."

Embrace a True Identity:
"Glorious Father"

The phrase "glorious Father" indicates our relationship to God and answers the question, "Why are we made for more?" We are made for more because we are children of God. For years I identified myself not by my relationship with God but by my circumstances. I was ...

Lysa, the broken girl from a broken home.

Lysa, the girl rejected by her father.

Lysa, the girl sexually abused by a grandfather figure.

Lysa, the girl who walked away from God after the death of her sister.

Lysa, the girl who had an abortion after a string of bad relationships.

Then one day I read a list of who God says I am. I took that list of Scriptures and started to redefine my identity. What a stark contrast to the way I saw myself. I finally realized I didn't have to be defined by my circumstances. Instead, I could live in the reality of who my glorious heavenly Father says I am:

Lysa, the forgiven child of God. (Romans 3:24)

Lysa, the set-free child of God. (Romans 8:1–2)

Lysa, the accepted child of God. (1 Corinthians 1:2)

Lysa, the holy child of God. (1 Corinthians 1:30)

Lysa, the made-new child of God. (2 Corinthians 5:17)

Lysa, the loved child of God. (Ephesians 1:4)

Lysa, the close child of God. (Ephesians 2:13)

Lysa, the confident child of God. (Ephesians 3:12)

Lysa, the victorious child of God (Romans 8:37)

I was made to be set free, holy, new, loved, and confident. Because of this, I can't allow myself to partake in anything that negates my true identity. Be it a relationship in which someone makes me feel less than my true identity or a vicious food cycle that leaves me defeated and imprisoned, I must remember I was made for more.

Living in victory tastes sweeter than any unhealthy delicacy.

The truth of my identity as a child of God empowers me to believe that living in victory tastes sweeter than any unhealthy delicacy.

Find the Deeper Reason:
"So that You May Know Him Better"

Did you catch the real reason we need to keep asking for wisdom and revelation and the real reason for embracing our true identity? It's not just so we can feel better about ourselves. It's not just to help us make healthier choices. It's not even to help us operate as victorious children of God. And it's certainly not so we can slip into smaller jeans and lose the muffin top, although these are all wonderful benefits.

The real reason for grounding ourselves in the truth that we are made for more is "so that you may know him better." The more we operate in the truth of who we are and the reality that we were made for more, the closer to God we'll become.

I don't know about you, but this one benefit alone is worth all the effort, struggle, and sacrifice a healthy eating journey requires. As many times as I've felt this is such an unfair thing to have to deal with—especially when I watch my naturally skinny friends eat whatever they want and never gain an ounce—I can now see this as somewhat of a privilege.

I know that sounds strange and a bit counterintuitive, so I'll cover this more in later chapters. But there is a deeper purpose behind our disciplined commitment. Making this connection—between being made for more and getting to know God better—helps this whole adventure be less about food and exercise and lifestyle choices and more about embracing a chance for deep and wonderful connections with God. And isn't that the greatest part of being made for more?

Discover a Hope and Power Like No Other:
"That the Eyes of Your Heart May Be Enlightened"

Isn't this an interesting phrase that comes next, "that the eyes of our heart may be enlightened" to the hope and power that is available to us? *Enlightened* literally means "to shed light upon."[3] In other words, the apostle Paul asks that light be shed upon our hearts so we can more clearly recognize the hope and power available to us.

We would do well to pray for the eyes of our hearts to be enlightened to this hope and power. Too many times, we try to muster up the gumption to make changes in our lives on our own. And it doesn't take long for the dark feelings of discouragement, disillusionment, and defeat to fill our hearts.

It is crucial to have a hope and a power beyond ourselves. We are made for the same hope and power that raised Christ from the dead. We've covered Ephesians 1:17 – 19a, but we must look at the rest of verse 19 and also verse 20. "That power is like the working of his mighty strength, which he exerted in Christ when he raised him from the dead and seated him at his right hand in the heavenly realms" (Ephesians 1:19 – 20). This is the power available to us! The same power that raised Jesus from the dead. It may not feel like we have this power, but we do. And each time we proclaim, "I am made for more," I pray all the power-packed truths within that statement rush into our hearts and keep us enlightened.

We were made for more than excuses and vicious cycles. We can taste success. We can experience truth. We can choose to stay on the path of hard work and perseverance. We can build one success on top of another. We can keep "made for more" at the top of our minds and on the tips of our tongues. And our eating habits can be totally transformed as we keep asking, embrace our true identity, find the deeper reason for claiming that identity, and operate in the hope and power that's like no other.

Personal Reflections

1. "I was made for more" is a spiritual truth that unlocks great power for Christians (page 51). When you think of your past failures and your current struggles with food, how do you hope this truth might help you?

2. When you introduce yourself to someone you don't know, how do you define yourself? By your family relationships (as a wife, mother, daughter, aunt)? By a professional title, or lack of one? By where you live or go to church? What might your introduction reveal about how you understand your own identity?

3. Lysa describes how she once defined her identity by her circumstances: Lysa, the broken girl from a broken home; Lysa, the girl rejected by her father; Lysa, the girl sexually abused by a grandfather figure. Have you ever felt your identity was defined by your circumstances? If you were to describe your identity as Lysa did, what would be on your list?

4. Take a moment to review the following list of statements, inserting your name before each one. How does this understanding of how God sees you impact the circumstance-based view of your identity you listed in response to question 3?

_____, the forgiven child of God. (Romans 3:24)

_____, the set-free child of God. (Romans 8:1–2)

_____, the accepted child of God. (1 Corinthians 1:2)

_____, the holy child of God. (1 Corinthians 1:30)

_____, the made-new child of God. (2 Corinthians 5:17)

_____, the loved child of God. (Ephesians 1:4)

_____, the close child of God. (Ephesians 2:13)

_____, the confident child of God. (Ephesians 3:12)

_____, the victorious child of God. (Romans 8:37)

5. Refer back to page 51 or your Bible. Reread Ephesians 1:17–20 and reflect on the key themes of the passage using the questions below.

   • *Be persistent: "I keep asking."* Do you have any reservations about asking God for wisdom and power each day to help you on this journey? How do you hope persistent prayer might help you?

   • *Embrace a true identity: "Glorious Father."* With what untruths about your identity have you struggled? How might your life change if you could embrace the truth of your identity as a child of God?

   • *Find the deeper reason: "So that you may know him better."* How might God use your journey toward healthy eating as a way to help you get to know Him better?

   • *Discover a hope and power like no other: "That the eyes of your heart might be enlightened."* To what degree do you feel like everything depends on you — your willpower and determination? A little, a lot? To what degree do you believe that the same power that raised Jesus from the dead is also available to help you? A little, a lot? As you reflect back on each day, how will you know whether you relied on your own strength or leaned into God's strength?

Growing Closer to God

Have you ever vulnerably shared your heart only to have someone slam your intentions and make you feel foolish? I was once at a conference doing a question-and-answer session when someone asked, "How do you grow close to God?"

Great question. Possible answers swirled about in my mind. I didn't want to give a trite answer complete with the typical checklist: Go to church. Don't cuss. Read the Bible. Pray. Give to the poor.

Those are all great things. I do believe doing those things pleases God. But simply checking those things off a list and then sitting back waiting for closeness to God to come won't happen. God can't be reduced to a checklist.

And might I dare add, growing closer to God has a whole lot less to do with any action we might take and a whole lot more to do with positioning our hearts toward His. It's what I call intentionally positioning ourselves to experience God—and the posture we are to take might surprise most well-meaning Christ seekers and followers.

> *Growing closer to God has a whole lot less to do with any action we might take and a whole lot more to do with positioning our hearts toward His.*

The posture isn't standing with our hands up high or arms outstretched. The posture is the lowest possible position in which we can put ourselves with empty hands and eager hearts. In other words, communicating with our intentions, our attitudes, and even our body language that we are willing to deny ourselves.

So, back to that question I was asked, "How do you grow close to God?"

I answered, "By making the choice to deny ourselves something that is permissible but not beneficial. And making this intentional sacrifice for the sole purpose of growing closer to God. After all, Jesus Himself said, 'If anyone would come after me, he must deny himself and take up his cross daily and follow me' [Luke 9:23]."

By way of example, I shared how right now I'm intentionally sacrificing sugar and processed things that turn into sugar in my body once consumed. Yes, I am doing it to get healthy. But the deeper reason for choosing to purify myself is to help me grow closer to God.

My answer was real, vulnerable, and honest. Maybe a little too honest. The women in the audience gasped when I said I'm in a season of sacrificing sugar. It wasn't two seconds later that a conference attendee grabbed the audience microphone and blurted out, "Well, if Jesus called Himself the bread of life, I can't see how sugar and processed carbs are bad at all!"

The audience erupted with laughter.

I forced a smile but I felt smaller than an ant. No, I take that back. Smaller than a wart on the end of an ant's nose. And that's pretty small.

They didn't get it.

Or maybe I didn't get it. Was I just a foolish, Jesus-chasing girl who mistakenly believed my desires to please Him with this food battle would somehow help me grow closer to Him?

Yes, I want to lose weight. But this journey is so much more than just that. It really is about learning to tell myself no and learning to make wiser choices daily. And somehow becoming a woman of self-discipline honors God and helps me live the godly characteristic of self-control. The fruit of the Spirit (the evidence of God's Spirit being in you) is a list of godly characteristics: love, joy, peace, patience, kindness, goodness, faithfulness, gentleness and self-control (Galatians 5:22). In the end, pursuing self-control does help my heart feel closer to Jesus and more pure to receive what He wants for me each day ... instead of clogged with guilty feelings for my poor choices.

But self-control is hard. We don't like to deny ourselves. We don't think it's necessary. We make excuses and declare, "That's nice for you, but I could never give that up." And if we're relying on ourselves, that's true. But there's another level to self-control that too few of us find. Before the apostle Paul lists the fruit of the Spirit in his letter to the churches in Galatia, he describes a power available to us that goes way beyond self-control: "So I say, *live by the Spirit*, and you will not gratify the desires of the sinful nature" (Galatians 5:16, emphasis added). In other words, live with the willingness to walk away when the Holy Spirit nudges you and says, "That food choice is permissible but not beneficial—so don't eat it." Not *sinful*—please hear me on this. Food isn't sinful. But when food is what Satan holds up in front us and says, "You'll never be free from this battle. You will always bounce from feeling deprived when you're dieting to feeling guilty when you're splurging. Victory isn't possible. You aren't capable of self-control with food," we must see that its inappropriate consummation can be his lure to draw our heart into a place of defeat. For others it will be sex outside marriage, the inappropriate consumption of alcohol, illegal drugs, or some other physical means.

> *Becoming a woman of self-discipline honors God and helps me live the godly characteristic of self-control.*

Of course, the obvious question then is how can we tune into these nudges of the Holy Spirit? How can we "live by the Spirit"?

First, we have to know where the Spirit is and what He gives us. If we know Jesus as our personal Savior, the Bible teaches that we have the Holy Spirit living in us: "And if the Spirit of him who raised Jesus from the dead is living in you, he who raised Christ from the dead will also give life to your mortal bodies through his Spirit, who lives in you" (Romans 8:11). Not only does the Spirit live in us, but He is active and infuses power to our lives that is beyond what we could possibly muster up on our own.

Now then, how do we live by this Spirit and heed His voice of wisdom and caution? Here's what the apostle Paul says: "Since we live by the Spirit, let us keep in step with the Spirit" (Galatians 5:25). In other words, we read the Bible with the intention of putting into practice what we read while asking the Holy Spirit to direct us in knowing how to do this.

I often pray this prayer: "I need wisdom to make wise choices. I need insight to remember the words I've read in Scripture. I need power beyond what I can find on my own." It's not a magic prayer. I still have to make the choice to walk away from the source of my temptation. And making that choice is sometimes really hard; I won't deny that.

Like when I'm in line at Starbucks. The barista takes my coffee order and then waves her hand like an enticing wand directing my attention to a case full of the delights that make a girl's taste buds dance. Seriously dance. Like the rumba, tango, and a snappy little quick step all in a row. My taste buds dance around while begging like a small child in the candy aisle.

"Would you like something to go with your coffee?" she asks.

Of course I'd like something—I'd like two or three somethings! And I'll be completely honest, it's in moments like these that I want to ask Eve to clarify one simple thing. Please tell me that something got lost in translation and what was really dangling from that tree limb all those years ago were treats like this. I'm just saying.

Anyhow. Like I said, it's not easy. It's not easy relying on the Holy Spirit to direct us into wise choices. It's not easy to dare to actually live a life in which we put Scripture to action. Especially Scriptures about self-control. It's not easy but it *is* possible.

We serve a compassionate God. A God who knew food would be a major stumbling block in our all-out pursuit of Him. Literally, issues with food can hold us back in our calling and our commitment to Christ. So, He's given us great gifts in the Holy Spirit, Jesus, and the Bible to help us. Let's look at two specific aspects of faith—our calling and our commitment—that God warns us must not be allowed to be eclipsed by food.

Our Calling

Whenever we feel defeated by an issue, it can make us feel unable to follow God completely. Sometimes this would haunt me and make me feel insecure in my ministry to women. Have you ever felt this way in your struggle with food? I bet you never dreamed the story of the Samaritan woman might provide some very sweet encouragement.

If you've attended many Christian women's conferences, you've probably heard the story of the Samaritan woman told from just about every possible angle. I'll admit, if I hear someone start to speak about her at a conference, my brain begs me to tune out and day-dream about tropical places or items I need to add to my Target list.

It's not that I don't like her story. I do. It's just that I've heard it so many times I find myself doubting there could possibly be any-thing fresh left to say about it. But in all my years of hearing about the Samaritan woman, reading her story and feeling like I know it, I missed something. Something really big.

Right smack dab in the middle of one of the longest recorded interactions Jesus has with a woman, He starts talking about food. Food! And I'd never picked up on it before. Somehow, in all this exposure to her story, I missed Jesus' crucial teaching that spiritual nourishment is more important than even physical nourishment. He says, "My food . . . is to do the will of him who sent me and to finish his work" (John 4:34). And then He goes on to say, "I tell you, open your eyes and look at the fields! They are ripe for harvest" (v. 35). There is a bigger plan here! Don't get distracted by physical food. Don't think physical food can satisfy the longing of your soul. Only Jesus can do this. Our souls were created to crave Him and love others to Him. See, there are many people waiting to hear the message of your calling. Don't get stuck in defeat and held back from it.

In the midst of offering salvation to the Samaritan woman, Jesus seems to wander off on this tangent about food. But it's not a tangent at all. Actually, it fits perfectly. It all goes back to the spiritual malnutrition we talked about in the introduction. Specifically, it's about trying to use food to fill not only the physical void of our stomachs but also the spiritual void of our souls. Here's the problem with that:

Food can fill our stomachs but never our souls.

Possessions can fill our houses but never our hearts.

Sex can fill our nights but never our hunger for love.

Children can fill our days but never our identities.

Jesus wants us to know only He can fill us and truly satisfy us. He really wants us to know that.

Only by being filled with authentic soul food from Jesus — following Him and telling others about Him — will our souls ever be truly satisfied. And breaking free from consuming thoughts about food allows us to see and pursue our calling with more confidence and clarity.

Our Commitment

I love God. I've loved God for a long time. But it took God quite a while to get my attention with my food issues. One of the things He used to get my attention in a very powerful way is pointing out things in the Bible I'd never really noticed before. The book of Philippians was where I noticed something very significant for the first time.

Philippians is often called the book of joy. However, there is not a lot of candy-coated joy tucked amongst some verses many of us have quoted for years. This section of Scripture starts off easy enough:

> But one thing I do: Forgetting what is behind and straining toward what is ahead, I press on toward the goal to win the prize for which God has called me heavenward in Christ Jesus. All of us who are mature should take such a view of things. And if on some point you think differently, that too God will make clear to you. Only let us live up to what we have already attained. (Philippians 3:13 – 16)

Love those verses. I want to forget what is behind! I want to press on toward the goal! I want to win the prize! I want to be mature! So, we clap our hands at the end of that message and promise to do some prize-winning pressing on for Jesus.

But wait. Don't file out of class just yet. If we look just a tad further in this chapter we'll find a telling verse about food:

> For, as I have often told you before and now say again even with tears, many live as enemies of the cross of Christ. Their destiny is destruction, their god is their stomach, and their glory is in their shame. Their mind is on earthly things. (Philippians 3:18 – 19)

Oh dear. Those are some stinging words. Toe-stubbing words. Words that don't exactly make us want to stand up and clap. But they are there and we must pay attention.

When the apostle Paul says, "their god is their stomach," he means that food can become so consuming that people find themselves ruled by it. To make that practical for the here and now, if we find that certain foods are impossible to walk away from — we can't or won't deny ourselves an unhealthy choice in order to make a healthier choice — then it's a clue we are being ruled by this food on some level. Being ruled by something other than God diminishes our commitment and will make us feel increasingly distant from Him.

Being ruled by anything other than God is something God takes quite seriously. And so should I.

Being ruled by anything other than God is something God takes quite seriously. And so should I. I don't want to live as an enemy to the cross of Christ. In other words, I don't want to live resistant to the power Christ's death and resurrection provides for me just because I can't walk away from my unhealthy cravings.

Thankfully, Paul's words to the Philippians don't end in verse 19. There's good news:

> But our citizenship is in heaven. And we eagerly await a Savior from there, the Lord Jesus Christ, who, by the power that enables him to bring everything under his control, will transform our lowly bodies so that they will be like his glorious body. (Philippians 3:20 – 21)

Now I can clap again. I want His power to help me bring everything — *everything* — under His control. I want my lowly body to be transformed. I want to be in the process of becoming more and more like Jesus. Yes, that makes me clap. It reestablishes that God, not food, is who is in control of me. That helps keep me undivided in my commitment to Him.

So, is this eating healthier journey really something that can help us grow closer to God?

Yes, I believe so. I stand by the answer I gave at the conference that day. And while making the intentional choice to deny myself unhealthy food options probably isn't the most popular route to growing closer to God, it is a route nonetheless. A thrilling, hard, practical, courageous spiritual journey with great physical benefits.

Personal Reflections

1. What is your response to the idea that we grow closer to God when we deny ourselves something that is permissible but not beneficial? Have you ever had an experience of denying yourself that helped you to grow closer to God? Do you believe this could be true for you in your battle with food?

2. The apostle Paul lists self-control among the fruit of the Spirit (Galatians 5:22). Are there areas of life in which you experience self-control and feel that your self-discipline and wise choices honor God? For example, in your spending decisions or how you manage your time? What insights about your strengths in those areas might help you to honor God and grow in self-control with your food choices?

3. Have you ever had the experience of the Holy Spirit nudging you in connection with your food choices? If so, what was that like? If not, how do you hope the Holy Spirit might help you now?

4. As Christians, our calling—and our source of spiritual nourishment—is to do God's will and finish His work (John 4:34). To what degree have consuming thoughts about food impacted your ability to pursue your calling and receive spiritual nourishment?

5. Would you say you are spiritually well fed, spiritually malnourished, or somewhere in between? Have you ever tried to use food to satisfy your feelings of spiritual hunger? What was the result?

6. If we find certain foods impossible to walk away from, this is a clue that we are being ruled by food on some level. Are there foods you can't or won't deny yourself in order to make a healthier choice? Why are these foods especially important to you? What thoughts and feelings arise when you think about potentially giving them up?

7

I'm Not Defined
by the Numbers

A few years ago, I was in an exercise class when the gal next to me leaned over and started to tell me that she'd spent the weekend with her sister. They'd had a good time but she came away concerned. It seems this sister had gained quite a bit of weight. I was half listening and half straining to lift my aching legs and crunch my screaming stomach. Suddenly I snapped to attention when she quipped, "I mean I can hardly believe it. I think my sister now weighs like 150 pounds."

I didn't know whether to laugh out loud or just keep my hilarious little secret to myself. The scandalous weight that horrified my workout friend was the exact number that had greeted me that very morning on my scale. And I was standing on one foot just in case that might slightly reduce the number.

About this time the exercise instructor directed us to grab our jump ropes, which abruptly ended the "overweight" sister conversation. But for the rest of the class, I couldn't wipe the smile off my face. I so desperately wanted to yell out three glorious words: "I AM FREE!" In that moment I had a small moment of victory over an identity disorder I'd battled for a very long time.

Like many women, I'd struggled with a flawed perception of myself. My sense of identity and worth were dependent on the wrong things—my circumstances or my weight or whether I yelled at the kids that day or what other people thought of me. If I sensed I wasn't measuring up, I kicked into either withdrawal mode or fix-it mode. Withdrawal mode made me pull back from relationships, fearing others' judgments. I built walls around my heart to keep people at a distance. Fix-it mode made me overanalyze other people's every word and expression looking for ways to manipulate their opinions to be more pleasing toward me. Take, for example, the crazy question I asked my husband every time I felt insecure while getting ready in the morning: "Does this make me look fat?"

This question had nothing to do with my outfit. It was an attempt to get him to say something, anything to make me feel better about myself. I could manipulate a compliment but, in the end, I still felt so empty.

Like many women, I'd struggled with a flawed perception of myself. My sense of identity and worth were dependent on the wrong things.

Both of these are crazy modes to be in.

So, I found great joy in realizing that my workout buddy's statement hadn't rattled me. I wasn't at my goal weight, but I was in the process of investing wisely in my health and in my spiritual growth. I had been diligently filling my heart and mind with God's truths during this journey and these truths were protecting me. In this moment, I could feel the Holy Spirit filling me with a calm reassurance. And it felt absolutely great to say to myself, "One hundred and fifty pounds isn't where I want to be, but it's better than where I started. It's tangible evidence of progress—and progress is good!"

I got a faint remembrance of some verses from Isaiah I'd recently marked in my Bible. Later, I looked them up and, though God was clearly talking to a ruler who probably had very different struggles than me, I found the words amazingly comforting. Here is what I heard God saying to me through the words He spoke to Isaiah:

"I will go before you ... *I [God] knew this comment would be made in exercise class this morning.*

... and will level the mountains ... *and that's why the Holy Spirit prompted you to remember these exact verses, even if only faintly, to protect you from what could have been a huge hurt to your heart.*

I will break down gates of bronze and cut through bars of iron ... *I will break through the lies that could have imprisoned you and made you doubt your true worth.*

I will give you the treasures of darkness, riches stored in secret places ... *In the most unlikely places I will bless your efforts and reward your perseverance with small indications of your victory.*

... so that you may know that I am the LORD, the God of Israel, who summons you by name" ... *I love you, Lysa. I loved you when you weighed almost 200 pounds. I loved you at 167. I love you at 150. I love you and no number on the scale will ever change that. I'm not taking you on this journey because I need you to weigh less. I am taking you on this journey because I desire for you to be healthy in every sense of the word. I know your name, Lysa. Now, rest in the security of My name and all that it means to your identity.* (Isaiah 45:2–3)

Do you see now why it's so important to fill our hearts and minds with God's words and how vital it is to make His truth the foundation not only for our identity but how we deal with food? The Holy Spirit uses God's words stored up inside us to nudge us, remind us, redirect us, empower us, and lead us on to victory. I wish I could give you a more definitive formula. Something a little more packaged and step-by-step and not so reliant on having to make a choice to listen to the Holy Spirit.

But one thing I can assure you: God wants to be in communication with us. And, as I said in the previous chapter, if you dedicate this journey to God, He promises the Holy Spirit will be with you every step of the way. And that means you have access to a power beyond what you can muster up on your own.

So, because of God's truth, this Jesus-loving girl wasn't defeated by my workout friend's remark. I didn't inwardly chastise myself for not loving raw veggie sticks of the green and orange variety. I didn't melt into a puddle of tears. My mind didn't start racing for where I might find the next greatest fad diet, one that would work a little quicker than my no-sugar, portion-control, spiritual journey.

This conversation about a 150-pound sister didn't define me in any way. I simply chuckled and moved on while humming that song from the animated movie *Shark Tale*, "I Like Big Butts and I Cannot Lie." It was truly a glorious life moment for me. I couldn't put my finger on the exact point at which I finally got past the insecurities that had haunted me for years. But this interaction was living proof I was finally on a healing path.

In the previous chapter we talked about growing closer to God by learning the powerful principle of denying ourselves things that distract us and hold us back from following. But here's another step for growing closer to God that we cannot miss: we grow closer to God as we learn to look and act more and more like Him. The Bible calls this participating in His divine nature. Not only do our actions need to reflect the self-control the Holy Spirit affords us, but our sense of identity needs to reflect His presence in our lives as well. Here's how the apostle Peter presents this truth:

> His divine power has given us everything we need for life and godliness through our knowledge of him who called us by his own glory and goodness. Through these he has given us his very great and precious promises, so that through them you may participate in the divine nature and escape the corruption in the world caused by evil desires.
>
> For this very reason, make every effort to add to your faith

goodness; and to goodness, knowledge; and to knowledge, self-control; and to self-control, perseverance; and to perseverance, godliness; and to godliness, brotherly kindness; and to brotherly kindness, love. For if you possess these qualities in increasing measure, they will keep you from being ineffective and unproductive in your knowledge of our Lord Jesus Christ. But if anyone does not have them, he is nearsighted and blind, and has forgotten that he has been cleansed from his past sins.

Therefore, my brothers, be all the more eager to make your calling and election sure. For if you do these things, you will never fall, and you will receive a rich welcome into the eternal kingdom of our Lord and Savior Jesus Christ. (2 Peter 1:3–11)

That's a lot of text, so let me summarize the principles in these verses that relate to our struggles with food and identity:

- God's divine power has given us everything we need to experience victory in our struggles.
- We are to reflect a divine nature — a secure identity in Christ — which helps us escape the corruption of the world and avoid evil desires.
- It is through biblical promises that we find the courage to deny unhealthy desires.
- Getting healthy is not just about having faith, goodness, and knowledge. We have to add to that foundation by choosing to be self-controlled and choosing to persevere even when the journey gets really hard.
- These qualities keep us from being ineffective and unproductive in our pursuit of healthy eating and, even more importantly, in our pursuit of growing closer to God.
- If we make the choice to be Jesus girls who offer our willingness to exercise self-control and perseverance to the glory of God, we can lose weight, get healthy, and walk in

confidence that it is possible to escape the cycle of losing and gaining back again. We can be victorious. We can step on the scale and accept the numbers for what they are—an indication of how much our body weighs—and not an indication of our worth.

May I just repeat that last little line? Maybe I should repeat it one hundred times. And all that repeating wouldn't be because I want to drive this truth home to you. It would be because I want to drive this truth home to myself.

I am a Jesus girl who can step on the scale and see the numbers as an indication of how much my body weighs and not as an indication of my worth.

I am a Jesus girl who can step on the scale and see the numbers as an indication of how much my body weighs and not as an indication of my worth.

Can we say it one more time?

I am a Jesus girl who can step on the scale and see the numbers as an indication of how much my body weighs and not as an indication of my worth.

We can step on the scale and accept the numbers for what they are—an indication of how much our body weighs—and not an indication of our worth.

Okay, now I'm starting to feel like an overly peppy cheerleader. But, sister, may I encourage you to let the truths of this chapter sink into the deep places of your heart? If you are like me, you've got places where parents, peers, friends, and foes have purposely or inadvertently hurt you with their comments. And sometimes those comments rattle around in your heart and mind and chip away at your worth.

That day in the gym, I could have let the words, "I can hardly believe it. She must weigh like 150 pounds" bump around and cause great damage. Instead, I took that comment and held it up to the truths the Holy Spirit was whispering. Like the apostle Peter said, we have been given everything we need for life and godliness. My classmate's inadvertent statement was not life and it was not godly. Therefore, I didn't have to internalize it. I could leave it on the gym floor and walk away.

That statement didn't belong to me. That statement wasn't my issue. I had a choice to make. I could feed that comment and let it grow into an identity crusher; or I could see it for what it was, a careless comment. Just like I can make the choice to leave the cookies in the bakery case and the chips on the grocery store shelf, I could make the choice to walk away from that remark. That's what the apostle Paul is talking about when he says, "We demolish arguments and every pretension that sets itself up against the knowledge of God, and we take captive every thought to make it obedient to Christ" (2 Corinthians 10:5).

We can literally say to a comment or a thought that presents itself to us, "Are you true? Are you beneficial? Are you necessary?" And if the answer is no, then we don't open the door of our heart. We make the choice to walk away from the comment and all the negative thoughts it could harvest if we let it in.

I love these verses. I love these truths. I love my identity as a Jesus girl. And I love not being defined by numbers.

Personal Reflections

1. When she felt like she didn't measure up, Lysa says she kicked into withdrawal mode or fix-it mode. What mode do you kick into when you feel like you don't measure up?

2. Lysa describes how God used a passage from Isaiah to encourage her and affirms how much God wants to be in

communication with us. If you could clearly hear God's words to you throughout the day, what kind of things would you hope you might hear Him say? What, specifically, would you like to hear Him say when you are struggling with food choices or issues related to your weight?

3. The apostle Peter writes that God's "divine power has given us everything we need for life and godliness" (2 Peter 1:3). In other words, with God's power we have everything we need to experience victory in our struggles. Do you feel you have everything you need from God in order to overcome your struggles with food? Or is this one of those truths that looks good on Bible paper but doesn't seem to impact your everyday life? How might your relationship to food change if you could fully embrace this truth?

4. "I am a Jesus girl who can step on the scale and see the numbers as an indication of how much my body weighs and not as an indication of my worth" (page 74). How do the numbers on the scale impact your self-worth? Is Lysa's statement one you can make with full confidence or is it something you aspire to but haven't quite reached?

5. What self-defeating thoughts or hurtful comments from others routinely run through your mind when it comes to food and your weight? What insights and perspective do you gain when you scrutinize them with these questions:

• Is this true?

• Is this beneficial?

• Is this necessary?

Making Peace with the Realities of My Body

I have a high school memory that haunted me for years. There was a boy over whom I was completely smitten. In today's language, teens would say I was crushin'.

Anyhow, I remember when the lights dimmed at school dances and somewhere between "My Sharona" and "Walk Like an Egyptian," inevitably came the sounds of Hall and Oates, "Your Kiss Is on My List." I had a list and he was at the very top ... you get the picture.

The only problem was that my crush had a list of his own and I not only wasn't at the top, but I hadn't even made the cut. To him, we were just friends. Put that little combo together and it was a formula for heartbreak.

Then came the moment that, more than twenty years later, I can still recall as if it happened yesterday. List Boy comes and sits beside me at the school dance. I try to play cool and act like I'm surprised to see him. Like I hadn't noticed him all night, though I had secretly kept a bead on his every move since he'd walked in. We exchange chitchat for a few minutes.

We are only speaking very simple words but inside of me a whole different thing is happening. My heart is beating out of my chest; my mind is leaping through pages of our future together—our first dance, our engagement, our wedding. Right as I'm getting around to naming our first three children, he drops a bomb on me.

Yeah, just like the song, "You Drop a Bomb on Me Baby, You Drop a Bomb on Me." He says he thinks I'm pretty cute, but it's too bad I have big ankles; otherwise we might be able to go out sometime.

"Excuse me? Did you just say I have big beautiful eyes? I know *ankles* and *eyes* don't sound much alike, but surely you didn't just say *ankles*?"

"No," he replies, "I actually said TANKLES."

Seriously, I could write one of those catchy *High School Musical* singsong-y songs and make millions from this horrid conversation. Picture some sweet, brace-faced girl's head, be-bopping back and forth, her grosgrain ribbons trying to stay on beat with her pony-tailed hair. Throw in a zit or two and less-than-model-like legs and the song would go something like this:

> *He loves me*
> *He loves me not.*
> *If it weren't for my tankles*
> *he'd think I was hot.*

Seriously ... TANKLES! Why couldn't he have kept this little opinion to himself? I could have just chalked up him never asking me out to my frizzy hair or my zits or my braces ... ALL OF THAT WOULD EVENTUALLY CHANGE. But my ankles? Tankles? Well, they would be my constant companion for life.

I eventually matured past my ankles bothering me every minute of every day. Just about the time where they were merely a weekly point of contention, I decided to have a little conversation with God about my ankles. I told Him this was a silly thing to bring up, but I really needed to have a better perspective on the whole tankle ankle situation.

I think the Lord had actually been eager for me to discuss this with Him. He was quick to answer my question with a question.

GOD: "Are you clumsy, Lysa?"

LYSA: "Yes, Lord. I am very clumsy."

GOD: "Have you ever twisted your ankle?"

LYSA: "Never."

GOD: "Wouldn't it bug you to constantly twist your ankle and be put out of commission?"

LYSA: "Yes, very much."

GOD: "Lysa, I have perfectly equipped you with ankles of strength and convenience. Be thankful."

The conversation wasn't as clear cut and back and forth as that. And no, I didn't audibly hear God's voice booming from heaven. But this is the message I got as I sat quietly and prayed about this. Maybe you could try having a similar "quiet time" with God about whatever your tankle equivalent is and see what He reveals to you.

I don't know a woman alive who is completely happy with her body. I don't know a woman alive who wakes up one day and says, "I have eaten healthy, I have exercised and, finally, I totally love the way I look." Not me. Probably not you. And not my friend Karen who lost over 100 pounds.

I don't know a woman alive who is completely happy with her body.

My friend Karen Ehman is one of my most favorite people to dialogue with about weight loss. Karen grew up with a single mom who truly loved her but couldn't always be as available as she wanted to be for her daughter. Many days, she'd try to fill in the gap of her absence by telling Karen she'd left a box of treats on the counter as she rushed off to work another shift.

Treats became Karen's comfort, what she'd turn to when she was lonely, sad, or stressed. This pattern became deeply ingrained in Karen and as the years went by, she ended up in what felt like an impossibly obese state. Through a series of medical scares and reality checks, Karen joined Weight Watchers and lost 100 pounds. And for three years, she was able to stick with it and keep the weight off.

Then her husband lost his job. They had to sell their home. Other stresses mounted and suddenly everything started spinning out of control. Suddenly, her old patterns of comfort seemed appealing again. Plus, being at her goal weight and still having to watch what she ate without the reward of watching the scale numbers go down wasn't as fun. What started as one treat turned into many and then turned into reverting back to those old, deeply ingrained habits. Five extra pounds turned into thirty and Karen felt the old pangs of defeat tempting her to make a complete reversal of all her progress.

It was time to get serious again, but boy was it hard the second time around. She knew some things would have to be different this time, the biggest being shifting her motivation from the delight of seeing the diminishing numbers on the scale to the delight of obedience to God.

On one of her "Weight Loss Wednesday" blog posts she wrote something I found incredibly insightful and profound. It brings together the theme of the last chapter about not being defined by the numbers with the theme of this chapter about making peace with our bodies. Here's what Karen wrote:

> I was very hopeful as I hopped on the scale this morning. I kept track of my food, exercised five days at the gym for 30–45 minutes, and my jeans were zipping up much easier than expected. So, I whipped the scale out of its locked-down location (hopping on the scale more than once a week proves often to be detrimental to me) and it said ...
>
> I lost 1.8 pounds.
>
> A measly 1.8 pounds! What!?! I was sure it would say at least

two or maybe even three. I felt gypped. And I felt like running to the kitchen to make a frozen waffle or two so I could slather it with real butter, spread it with some Peter Pan, and douse it with a load of pure maple syrup to drown my sorrows.

Then I stopped and remembered what I felt the Lord saying this week.

Define your week by obedience, not by a number on the scale.

The scale does help measure our progress, but it can't tell us everything. It can't tell us if the problem is too much salt intake that is making us retain a pound or two of water. It can't tell us if we actually lost a pound of fat but gained more muscle from weight training. And (in my case this week), it can't tell us what time of the month it is and then give us automatic credit for the extra two pounds or so those glorious few days bring to us.

So, I had to stop and ask myself the following questions:

- Did I overeat this week on any day? No.
- Did I move more and exercise regularly? Yes.
- Do I feel lighter than I did at this time last Wednesday? Yes.
- Did I eat in secret or out of anger or frustration? No.
- Did I feel that, at any time, I ran to food instead of to God? Nope.
- *Before* I hopped on the scale, did I think I'd had a successful, God-pleasing week? Yep!

So, why oh why do I get so tied up in a stupid number? And why did I almost let it trip me up and send me to the kitchen for a 750-calorie binge? (Don't worry. I had a yogurt and tea instead.)

Sweet friends, we need to define ourselves by our obedience, not a number on the scale.

Okay?

Pinky promise?

Good.

We are all in this thing together.

And we *will* get the weight off, even if it is 1.8 pounds at a time![4]

I love what Karen says about defining ourselves by our obedience and not by a number on the scale—or, for me, what size my clothes are or how I feel when certain models from a certain company prance across my TV proclaiming Victoria has a secret. I could eat healthy and exercise until the cows come home and never look like Victoria or any of her friends.

Yes, eating healthy and exercising get our bodies into better shape, but we are never supposed to get the satisfaction our souls desire from our looks. Our looks are temporary; if we hitch our souls to this fleeting pursuit, we'll quickly become disillusioned. The only true satisfaction we can seek is the satisfaction of being obedient to the Lord.

I love the questions Karen tackled. What a great list of questions for me to ask when, though I'm at my goal weight, I try on a swimsuit and the glare of the fluorescent lights highlights a multitude of imperfections. Or when it's still necessary for me to wear Spanx with some of my dress pants. Or when my tankles remind me skirts aren't my best wardrobe option.

The body God has given me is good. It's not perfect nor will it ever be. But it is a gift for which I am thankful.

The body God has given me is good. It's not perfect nor will it ever be. I still have cellulite. I still have tankles. And though I eat healthy, there are no guarantees—I'm just as susceptible as the next gal to cancer or some other disease. But my body is a gift, a good gift for which I am thankful. Being faithful in taking care of this gift by walking according to God's plans gives me renewed strength to keep a healthy view of my body. And so, like the psalmist, I can pray this prayer of thanksgiving for the body I have and mean it:

Praise the LORD, O my soul; all my inmost being, praise his holy name. Praise the LORD, O my soul, and forget not all his benefits—who forgives all your sins and heals all your diseases, who redeems your life from the pit and crowns you with love and compassion, who satisfies your desires with good things so that your youth is renewed like the eagle's. (Psalm 103:1–5)

It's so easy to get laser focused on what we see as wrong with our bodies. I know it was this way with my ankles. I knew I could eat healthy and exercise the rest of my life and still have tankles. In the grand scheme of things, I know this is a shallow concern. But, if I allowed my brain to park in a place of dissatisfaction about any part of my body, it would give Satan just enough room to move in with his lie that strips me of motivation: "Your body is never going to look the way you want it to look, so why sacrifice so much? Your discipline is in vain." That's why I have to seek the Lord's perspective and, as Psalm 103 reminds us, "forget not all his benefits."

God hasn't cursed your body with certain flaws. He didn't curse my body with tankles. When I took time to ask Him, God revealed the benefit of my larger ankles. Oh what freedom! What redemption! What a sweet gift! What a settling satisfaction! And just as Psalm 103 affirms, God satisfies your desires "with good things so that your youth is renewed like the eagle's."

When I studied this verse and decided to rest in the reality of what a good gift my body is, for the first time in my life I thanked God for making me just the way He made me. I am able to look at airbrushed, skinny-ankled women on TV or in the magazines and be happy for that person without loathing myself.

I've found my beautiful. And I like my beautiful. I don't have to hold my beautiful up to others with a critical eye of judgment. Like Ralph Waldo Emerson once said, "Though we travel the world over to find the beautiful, we must carry it with us or we find it not."[5]

Now, as the legendary radio commentator Paul Harvey used to say, here's the rest of the story. Had I possessed ankles that appealed to List Boy, danced, gotten engaged to and married him ... well, I would have missed out on an amazing man named Art, who loves me tankles and all.

Personal Reflections

1. We all have at least one physical feature we wish we could change. For some it might be a facial feature like the shape of one's nose; for others it could be breast size or body shape. For Lysa, it's "tankles." What is your tankle equivalent? What's your first memory of feeling embarrassed or ashamed by this aspect of your appearance? Are you now more or less at peace with this part of your body or is it still a source of painful dissatisfaction?

2. Karen Ehman describes how she learned to shift her motivation from the delight of seeing diminishing numbers on the scale to the delight of obedience to God (page 81). When you consider previous efforts to modify your eating habits, what experiences or accomplishments provided your greatest motivation to keep going? Did those motivations ever backfire or become demotivators?

3. Karen made practical her efforts to redefine progress by asking herself the questions listed below. As you review each question and reflect back on your eating over the past week, how would you assess your progress? Are there other questions you would like to add to the list?

   • Did I overeat this week on any day?

   • Did I move more and exercise regularly?

   • Do I feel lighter than I did at this time last week?

- Did I eat in secret or out of anger or frustration?
- Did I feel that, at any time, I ran to food instead of to God?
- Before I hopped on the scale, did I think I'd had a successful, God-pleasing week?

4. Lysa describes how it's possible to park our brains in a place of dissatisfaction about our bodies or to accept our bodies and thank God for making us just as we are. Place an X on the continuum below to describe your current feelings about your body.

My body is cursed with flaws.   My body is a good gift.

Imagine for a moment that the placement of the X above was made not by you but by someone you love — a child, a friend, a sister. How would the placement of the X make you feel? What would you want to say to this person? How might you pray for them? Are these things you could say to yourself, pray for yourself?

5. Lysa describes the freedom and redemption she felt when she discovered the benefits of her larger ankles (page 79). Have you ever thought about your physical flaws from this perspective? What might be the hidden benefits to the physical features you wish you did not have?

6. If someone offered to grant you one of the following wishes, which would you choose? How do you imagine your life might change as a result of either choice?

- Instant and painless cosmetic surgery to change one thing (like Lysa's tankles) about your physical appearance.
- A permanent reorientation of how you think and feel about your body that would enable you to say wholeheartedly, "I've found my beautiful. And I like my beautiful."

But Exercise Makes
Me Want to Cry

When I first started dating my exercise-loving husband, I hated to run. But I quickly got motivated when I discovered it was a fantastic way to spend more time with this man over whom I was completely smitten.

It's amazing how love can motivate us. He ran. I ran. We ran together. And while I loved spending this time with Art, I never did find a love for running.

On the first day of our honeymoon, Art woke up and cheerfully invited me to go on a run. "Now, why would I want to do that? I don't like to run. And now that we're married I see no need. I believe the only reason a person should sweat is if they're lying by the pool. Let's do that."

Art looked at me stunned.

Now, here's the crazy part. Before I met Art, I'd prayed for a husband who would motivate and encourage me to exercise. Have mercy, did God answer that prayer! And boy, did it cause some serious "growth opportunities" for us both.

It was such a battle for me. I would halfheartedly do something physical a couple of times a week, hating every minute of it. The most frustrating part was halfhearted efforts only produced mediocre results. Over the years, I started slipping further and further out of shape.

Eventually, I stood in front of the mirror trying to determine whether or not I should just resign myself to being out of shape. I wondered, *Have I reached an age and stage of life where losing weight and getting fit are impossible?*

Halfhearted efforts produce mediocre results.

The many extra pounds that had crept onto my body could easily be justified. After all, I've birthed three children. I even seemed to gain weight with the two we adopted. I'm very busy with them. This is my season of raising kids, not lifting weights. I'm too busy running carpools to run for exercise. But, in the quiet of my heart, I wasn't settled. The reality was I didn't feel good physically or emotionally. I cringed at the thought of having to undress in front of my husband. Not because he would judge me, but rather I'd be judging myself. Nothing can kill a romantic mood quicker than a woman's negative thoughts about herself. I would catch myself standing in front of the bathroom mirror in tears many mornings, lamenting over which pants could best hide my bulge. I cried out to God and admitted it was crazy to get emotional about my pants, for heaven's sake. I wanted to rise above this vain issue and be comfortable with who I was no matter what size. The tide of justifications would roll back in, only this time with a spiritual twist: *The world has sold us women a bill of goods that to be good we have to be skinny. I am too concerned with my spiritual growth to be distracted by petty issues such as weight and exercise. God loves me just the way I am.*

While the spiritual justifications also sounded good, in my heart I still wasn't settled. I knew my weight issue didn't have anything to do with me being spiritual or worldly. If I was honest with myself, my issue was plain and simple—a lack of self-control. I could sugarcoat it and justify it all day long, but the truth was I didn't have a weight problem; I had a spiritual problem. I depended on food for comfort more than I depended on God. And I was simply too lazy to make time to exercise.

Ouch. That truth hurt.

So, the day after Mother's Day a couple of years ago, I got up first thing in the morning and went running. Well, the word *running* should be used very loosely for what I actually did. I got out and moved my body quicker than I had in a long time. And you know what? I hated it. Exercise just made me want to cry.

It also made me hot and sticky. It made my legs hurt and my lungs burn. Nothing about it was fun until after I finished. But the feeling of accomplishment I felt afterward was fantastic! So, each day I would fight through the tears and excuses and make the effort to run.

At first I could only slowly jog from one mailbox to another—in a neighborhood where the houses are close together, thank you very much. Slowly, I started to see little evidences of progress. The key word here is *slowly*. Every day I asked God to give me the strength to stick with it this time. I'd tried so many other times and failed after only a few weeks. The more I made running about spiritual growth and discipline, the less I focused on the weight. Each lost pound was not a quest to get skinny but evidence of obedience to God.

One day, I went out for my version of a run and God clearly spoke to my heart. I often spent my exercise time talking with God, but today a clear command from God rumbled in my heart: "Run until you can't take another step. Do it not in your strength but in Mine. Every time you want to stop, pray for that struggling friend you just challenged not to give up and take your own advice—don't stop until I tell you to."

There have been many other times when God has given me clear directives to do things but never one that was this physically demanding. I had a record up to that point of running three miles, which I thought was quite stellar. For me, three miles seemed like a marathon. So, maybe God wanted me to run just slightly past the three-mile marker and rejoice in relying on His strength to do so. But as I reached that point in my run, my heart betrayed my aching body and said, "Keep going."

Each step thereafter, I had to pray and rely on God. The more I focused on running toward God, the less I thought about my desire to stop. And this verse from the Psalms came to life: "My flesh and my heart may fail, but God is the strength of my heart and my portion forever" (73:26).

The more I made exercise about spiritual growth and discipline, the less I focused on the weight. Each lost pound was not a quest to get skinny but evidence of obedience to God.

As I ran that day, I connected with God on a different level. I experienced what it meant to absolutely require God's faith to see something through. How many times have I claimed to be a woman of faith but rarely lived a life requiring faith? That day, God didn't have me stop until I ran 8.6 miles.

Hear me out here. It was *my* legs that took every step. It was *my* energy being used. It was *my* effort that took me from one mile to three to five to seven to 8.6. But it was *God's strength* replacing my excuses step by step by step.

For a mailbox-to-mailbox, crying-when-she-thought-of-exercising, allergic-to-physical-discipline kind of girl, it was a modern-day miracle. I broke through the "I can't" barrier and expanded the horizons of my reality. Was it hard? Yes. Was it tempting to quit? Absolutely. Could I do this in my own strength? Never. But this really wasn't about running. It was about realizing the power of God taking over my complete weakness.

I should also note that I went back to my standard three-mile track the next time I ran. But slowly I increased my daily runs to four miles and am very happy with that distance. Running 8.6 miles on a daily basis isn't realistic for me. But that one day, it was glorious. Especially because of what I discovered when I got home.

Since I'd been thinking of a verse from Psalms during my run, I grabbed my Bible as soon as I got home and opened it up to Psalm 86, in honor of my 8.6 miles.

Here is part of what I read: "Teach me your way, O LORD, and I will walk in your truth; give me an undivided heart, that I may fear your name. I will praise you, O LORD my God, with all my heart; I will glorify your name forever" (Psalm 86:11 – 12).

An undivided heart. That's what my whole journey in conquering my cravings was about. When it comes to my body, I can't live with divided loyalties. I can either be loyal to honoring the Lord with my body or loyal to my cravings, desires, and many excuses for not exercising. The apostle Paul taught the Corinthians about this two thousand years ago when he wrote: "Do you not know that your body is a temple of the Holy Spirit, who is in you, whom you have received from God? You are not your own; you were bought at a price. Therefore honor God with your body" (1 Corinthians 6:19).

I found the most interesting story in the Old Testament about how serious God is about people taking care of the temple entrusted to them. Before the Holy Spirit was given to us and our bodies became the temples for God's presence, God was present with His people in a house of worship called a temple. The book of Haggai describes how one of the first things God's people did when they returned from exile in Babylon was to rebuild the temple. They started with great enthusiasm and wonderful intentions but slowly slipped back into complacency and eventually stopped their work on the temple completely. Other things seemed more urgent, more appealing to work on. Here's how God responds:

> This is what the LORD Almighty says: "These people say, 'The time has not yet come for the LORD's house to be built.'"

Then the word of the LORD came through the prophet Haggai: "Is it a time for you yourselves to be living in your paneled houses, while this house remains a ruin?"

Now this is what the LORD Almighty says: "Give careful thought to your ways. You have planted much, but have harvested little. You eat, but never have enough. You drink, but never have your fill. You put on clothes, but are not warm. You earn wages, only to put them in a purse with holes in it."

This is what the LORD Almighty says: "Give careful thought to your ways. Go up into the mountains and bring down timber and build the house, so that I may take pleasure in it and be honored," says the LORD. (Haggai 1:2–8)

Oh, this reminds me just how divided my heart can be when it comes to taking care of my body, God's temple. Just like these people, I could so easily say, "I'm not in a season where it's feasible to take care of my body. I just can't find the time between the kids, my work responsibilities, running a home, paying the bills, and all the day-to-day activities. It's just not realistic for me to exercise."

But the Lord's strong caution is to "give careful thought to [our] ways" and to make time to "build the house" so that He may be honored. God's people neglected building the temple for ten years. Each year something else seemed to be more important. For years, I did the same thing with exercise. Something else was always a higher priority.

However, if I were really honest, I'd have to admit I made time for what I wanted to make time for. I wasn't giving careful thought to my ways. I wasn't making a plan to exercise each day and giving that time the same priority over more minor things. I always seemed to find time to watch a favorite TV show or chat with a friend on the phone. Just the same, the Jews who returned from Babylon obviously had time to do things they really wanted to do as well. They found the time and energy to put paneling up in their own homes while ignoring the home of the Lord.

There were consequences of failing to care for the Lord's temple: "Therefore, because of you the heavens have withheld their dew and the earth its crops" (Haggai 1:10). Now, I'm not saying God will cause bad things to happen to us if we don't exercise, but there are natural consequences for not taking care of our bodies. People who don't care for their bodies now will live with the consequences of those choices at some point. Be it more weight and less energy now or heart disease later, our choices matter both in the physical sense and the spiritual sense.

In the spiritual sense, when I'm not taking care of my body, I feel much more weighed down by my stress and problems. I have less energy to serve God and more thorny emotions to wade through when processing life.

Speaking of processing life, my friend Holly and I run together now just about every morning. While I can't say I'm always eager to jump out of bed and start running, I'm always glad I'm doing it once I've started. Not to mention how fantastic I feel when we finish. In addition to the benefit of exercising together, we also use that time to pray together, contemplate decisions, and talk about what God is teaching us.

May I admit something very strange to you? I'm actually thankful now I have a body and a metabolism that requires me to exercise. I've given careful thought to my ways and determined that taking care of my temple is a top priority. I schedule it. I'm held accountable to each day's appointment because I know Holly will be calling me if I don't show up. I've learned to embrace the benefits instead of resisting the hardship. And though I never thought I'd say this, I love the feeling of accomplishment running gives me each day. Even if everything else in my day falls apart, I can smile and say, "Yes, but with the Lord's help, I ran four miles this morning!"

Running may not be your thing. So, find what is. My mom loves to say the best kind of exercise is the kind you'll do. I agree. And while I fully realize my temple may not be God's grandest dwelling, I want to lift up to the Lord whatever willingness I have each day and dedicate my exercise as a gift to Him and a gift to myself. This one act undivides my heart and reminds me of the deeper purposes for moving my body.

My mom loves to say the best kind of exercise is the kind you'll do.

Now, might I share a quick funny about my temple not being the grandest of dwellings? While on vacation this past summer I went to the hotel gym. It was not the best workout situation because there was no air conditioning—and it was really hot. So, to help distract my brain from the pain I was about to endure while walk/jogging—we'll call it walogging—on the treadmill, I grabbed my husband's iPod. Wondering what kind of praise music he listens to while working out, I was touched when I saw a category of music called "Queen."

Awwwww, these must be songs about ME! Oh, I felt like I was about to read his diary, sneaky and giddy all at the same time as I hopped on that machine feeling more motivated by the minute.

Then the music started.

Now, let me state for the record, my husband loves him some Jesus. Yes, he does. But let me also state for the record that while you can take the boy out of high school, you cannot take the high school out of the boy's iPod.

Ahem.

The "praise" song about his "Queen" was—hold on, I'll let you brace yourself . . .

"Fat Bottomed Girls Make the Rockin' World Go 'Round."

The worst part of it all is by the time I realized what the song was saying, I had been humming the catchy tune out loud for all the exercise world to hear. Anyone familiar with the tune probably knew the words and got quite a laugh at my expense.

I'll let that picture soak into your brain for just a second. And that's all I have to say about that except that skirted bathing suits are a blessed invention.

Anyhow, today, you won't find me lamenting in front of the mirror. You'll find me out for a morning jog. You'll find me eating a sensible breakfast. You'll find I am twenty-six pounds lighter. While that's a wonderful benefit, you'll find what really makes me feel settled is that undivided heart thing—knowing that with God I'm able to say unreservedly, "I can! I will! I did!"

Indeed, it's amazing how love can motivate us—especially when it's God's unreserved love matched with our undivided heart.

Personal Reflections

1. What thoughts, emotions, or images come to mind when you think about exercise? Are your associations positive, negative, or a mix?

2. Lysa describes her experience of literally running on faith one day when God prompted her to keep running until He told her to stop. She ran 8.6 miles, 5.6 miles farther than she had ever run before. What experiences have you had that required faith you didn't think you had to see something through? What did you learn? How did it impact your relationship with God?

3. In what areas of life do you feel strong? For example, in your professional knowledge, your gifts of hospitality, your creative skills, your ability to pray for others, etc. Have you ever used these strengths to help someone who was weak or didn't know as much as you did? How might such experiences give you insights into what it means to allow God's power to take over your weaknesses, especially weaknesses with food and exercise?

4. "Teach me your way, O LORD, and I will walk in your truth; give me an undivided heart, that I may fear your name" (Psalm 86:11). When it comes to your body, what forces compete for your attention and loyalty? Do you feel torn between the desire to honor God and the desire to be loyal to cravings and excuses for not exercising? How do you imagine your life might be different if you had an undivided heart?

5. When you think about your schedule and daily demands, which of the following statements comes closest to describing how you feel about your time:

- Most of my time is within my control. I have a limited number of responsibilities or obligations that can't be changed but I am otherwise able to plan my own schedule.

- Some of my time is within my control. I have several responsibilities or obligations that can't be changed, but I do have pockets of time each week that I can use for things I want to do.

- Almost none of my time is within my control. My responsibilities and obligations are all-consuming right now. The only way I could add one more thing to my schedule is to skip what little sleep I manage to get each night.

How does your response help you understand your feelings about making time to exercise? On a scale of one to ten (one being very little and ten being a great deal), how much effort would it take to make time in your schedule for regular exercise (three to five times a week)?

6. Lysa says about exercise, "I've learned to embrace the benefits instead of resisting the hardship." Draw a line down the center of a piece of paper. On one side, list all the hardships of exercising; on the other side list all the benefits. Which list has more influence on you? Do you feel the benefits outweigh the hardships or vice versa? Can you imagine that it might be possible for you to embrace the benefits rather than resisting the hardship? Why or why not?

This Isn't Fair!

A big, huge piece of bakery deliciousness sat in front of me. It was a combination of three different desserts in one. One layer was cheesecake, one layer was ice cream cake, and in between both of those was a layer of brownie-like chocolate cake ... all drizzled with some kind of fudge icing that was literally calling my name.

This was served to me while Art and I were on that same special romantic vacation I mentioned in the previous chapter. The one where I found the song, "Fat Bottom Girls Make the Rockin' World Go 'Round." Yes, let's not go there again.

Saying "it's not fair" has caused many a girl to toss aside what she knows is right for the temporary thrill of whatever it is that does seem fair.

Anyhow, at the time, I was at the beginning of my no-sugar adventure. I'd been doing great at home but sitting there staring at that dessert was tough. I'd been dropped into a place that was teeming with bakery things my mind could not even conceive of, with my husband who could eat a pound of sugar a day and still look fit and trim.

I didn't want Art to miss out so I told him to please enjoy. "I'm fine," I said with a carefree smile. But inside a totally different dialogue was playing in my mind: "It's not fair!"

I think this is one of the biggest tricks Satan plays on us girls to get us to give into temptation.

Saying "it's not fair" has caused many a girl to toss aside what she knows is right for the temporary thrill of whatever it is that does seem fair. But the next day the sun will rise as it has a habit of doing every day. As each band of light becomes brighter and brighter, the realization of the choice she made the night before becomes clearer and clearer.

Guilt floods her body.

Questions fill her mind.

Self-doubt wrecks her confidence.

And then comes the anger. Anger at herself. Anger at the object of her desire. Anger even at a mighty God who surely could have prevented this.

It's not fair that others can have this, do this, act this way.

It's not fair that God won't let us eat of the fruit of the tree in the middle of the garden ... one little bit wouldn't be so bad, right?

It's not fair I can't buy that new thing I not only want but really feel I need. Just a little debt wouldn't be so bad, right?

It's not fair I have this body that requires I watch everything I eat when that girl eats junk and stays a size four. One piece of cheesecake wouldn't be so bad, right?

It's not fair that we can't have sex before we're married when we're so in love. Experimenting one time wouldn't be so bad, right?

Our flesh buys right into Satan's lie that it's not fair for things to be withheld from us. So we bite into the forbidden fruit and allow Satan to write "shame" across our heart.

Now, I realize a piece of cheesecake is a small compromise compared to a young girl losing her purity. But if one piece of dessert leads to two and that leads to other compromises, which leads to wrecking our whole healthy eating plan, then the downward spiral is quite similar.

And whether we are talking about having premarital sex or cheating on our diet, once we taste the forbidden fruit, we will crave it worse than we craved it before. Thereby giving temptation more and more power. And given enough power, temptation will consume our thoughts, redirect our actions, and demand our worship. Temptation doesn't take kindly to being starved.

I don't know what tempts you today. But I do know this vicious cycle and I'm here to give you hope that it is possible to conquer it. Just typing that sentence gives me chills. A few years ago, I wondered if it might ever be possible for me.

Our flesh buys right into Satan's lie that it's not fair for things to be withheld from us.

As I mentioned in an earlier chapter, the eating plan I chose was a no-sugar, balanced, healthy-carbs-and-protein plan. Which doesn't sound so bad until you realize sugar is in just about everything we enjoy eating. Breads, pasta, potatoes, rice, not to mention all things bakery-licious.

So, sitting at that special dinner during my special vacation, I started to have a little pity party and those words crept into my brain, "It's not fair."

In that instant, I squirmed in my chair and thought, *I'll just take one little bite ... maybe two ... I've been so good ... I even exercised this morning ... this is vacation ... everyone else is indulging ... oh my stars, what are you doing, Lysa?!*

The sugar was like a siren of mythical tales, luring the ships over to rocky coves that would inevitably dash and destroy them. The seduction was smooth and seemingly innocent.

But in that moment of temptation, I realized having a pity party was a clue I was relying on my own strength, a strength that has failed me before and would fail me again.

I had to grab hold of God's strength and the only way to do that was to invite His power into this situation. In this case, I gave

God control of the situation by mentally reciting the go-to script I mentioned in a previous chapter: "I am made for more. I am made for victory."

I recalled pieces of Scriptures I've tied to this go-to script and banked up in my heart. "I'm more than a conqueror." "With God all things are possible." "Let the peace of God reign in your heart." "Lead us not into temptation but *deliver* us from the evil one ..."

I realized having a pity party was I clue I was relying on my own strength, not God's.

The problem is, Satan hit me with a twist that left me momentarily vulnerable and shaky. "But this is a special time, Lysa. And special times deserve an exception to your normal parameters. It's not fair that you have to sacrifice. Look around you. No one else is sacrificing right now."

Poor me. This isn't fair. I've lived with this struggle for so long. This is a special time. I could just give in this once. Everyone else is doing it.

It's at this exact point when the dieter on vacation indulges. The virgin sleeps with her prom date. The girl on a debt reduction plan pulls her credit card back out for a big sale. The alcoholic skips AA and heads off to the bar for her friend's fortieth birthday instead. They may know they are made for more, but somehow Satan dissipates this truth with a rationalization: "Special times deserve special exceptions and anything else just isn't fair."

I needed a go-to script for this situation. So, I lowered my head and prayed, "God, I am at the end of my strength here. This is the moment I've got to sense Your strength stepping in. The Bible says Your power is made perfect in weakness. This would be a really good time for that truth to be my reality. Help me see something else besides this temptation looming so large in front of me it seems impossible to escape."

Suddenly a memory flashed across the screen of my mind. I was sitting on my back deck with my teenage son and his girlfriend having a deeply honest and gut-wrenching conversation. They had gotten into a bad situation and allowed things to go too far physically. While not every boundary line was crossed, they had crossed enough to scare them both. My advice to them was to think beyond the moment. Say out loud, "This feels good now, but how will I feel about this in the morning?"

That was it. I was challenged by the words and expectations I had placed on my son while not realizing how this same advice could be so powerful if applied to my area of struggle. I had my next go-to script and as I recited it, God's power filled in the gap of my weakness.

Soon, it was time to get up from the dinner table. I pushed back my chair, left the dessert untouched, and walked back to our room. And I've never felt so empowered in my life. Later, I looked up that verse about God's strength being a perfect match for my weakness:

Weakness is hard, but it doesn't have to mean defeat. It is my opportunity to experience God's power firsthand.

But he [Jesus] said to me, "My grace is sufficient for you, for my power is made perfect in weakness." Therefore I will boast all the more gladly about my weaknesses, so that Christ's power may rest on me. That is why, for Christ's sake, I delight in weaknesses, in insults, in hardships, in persecutions, in difficulties. For when I am weak, then I am strong. (2 Corinthians 12:9 – 10)

God's power is made perfect in weakness. This stirs my heart. Weakness is hard, but weakness doesn't have to mean defeat. It is my opportunity to experience God's power firsthand. Had I said yes to that one bite that first night of our vacation, there would have been more compromises. Compromise built upon compromise equals failure.

Instead, resisting temptation allowed promise upon promise to be built up in my heart, and that creates empowerment. This is God's power working through my weakness. I knew one day I would be empowered enough to take a couple of bites and walk away, but that day had not yet come.

I don't know what you might be struggling with today, but I can assure you that God is fair and just. There is a good reason we must face our temptations. The struggle to say no may be painful in the moment, but it is working out something magnificent within us.

For so long I've considered my struggles with weight a curse. The thought that this isn't fair doesn't happen only on vacation. It also happens when I watch my size-two friend eating handfuls of French fries and chocolate chip cookies while I'm eating yet another salad. How fair is that?

Have you ever felt this way? We aren't alone. Listen to what some of my blog friends said when I asked them about the "it's not fair" issue:

I have a skinny sister who can lose at the drop of a dime and does. It has always baffled me. I wonder if her DNA got all the family's willpower and high metabolism. It is very hard being the fattest in the family. — *Jessica*

How many times have I said this exact thing to my friends. Why do I struggle with this? Why can't I struggle with something else? How I've begged for God to remove this thorn from me. Yet, it's still there and I'm still here struggling. — *Lindsey*

Thank you for acknowledging this very real struggle! You're right, there are many way-worse things in this world. But this *is* still really hard for some of us (like me). I have even found myself jealous of other people's less visible struggles. I've wished that instead of being hooked on food, I could be hooked on cigarettes or alcohol. *What*?! I know that's ridiculous, but in my weakest, saddest, most frustrated moments, I believe the lie that everyone else — even people struggling with really hard things — have it better than me. —*Mary*

But, what if this battle with food isn't the curse we've always thought it to be? What if it's actually the very thing, if brought under control, that can lead us to a better understanding of God? What if we could actually get to the place where we thanked God for letting us face this battle because of the rich treasures we discovered on the battlefield?

> *What if this battle with food isn't the curse we've always thought it to be?*

My friend E. Titus sums up what I am discovering as well:

When I get all caught up in how unfair it is that my friend is skinny and doesn't have to work at it, how she can eat what she wants when she wants, and how much it stinks that I can't be like her, I remind myself that God didn't make me to be her. You see, He knew even before I was born that I could easily allow food to be an idol in my life, that I would go to food, instead of to Him, to fulfill my needs. And in His great wisdom, He created my body so that it would experience the consequences of such a choice, so that I would continually be drawn back into His arms. He wants me to come to Him for fulfillment, emotional healing, comfort — and if I could go to food for that and never gain an ounce, well then, what would I need God for?

There is such wisdom in my friend's perspective. Instead of parking her brain in a place where she constantly feels a struggle with food and weight issues, she's chosen a much healthier perspective.

The reality is, we all have things in our lives we have to learn to surrender, give up, sacrifice, turn away from. Back to my vacation example. Yes, my husband could eat all the desserts he wanted, but he has other areas in which he has to learn how to depend on God. Think of that skinny girl in your life who you've watched eating whatever she wants and thought how unfair that is. She may not struggle with her weight, but trust me, she has struggles. An anonymous comment on my blog gave vulnerable witness to this reality:

> I am one of the skinny girls, but don't mistake skinny for healthy. I battle depression and starvation, fight self-esteem issues from years of verbal abuse, the list seems endless. Little is just an image. But being little doesn't make a person any more happy or faithful or joyful. The struggles are the same (or at least similar), just in a different size package.

Life as a Christ follower will always be a learning process of depending less on our own strength and more on God's power. The Bible teaches that this "testing of [our] faith develops perseverance [which] must finish its work so that [we] may be mature and complete, not lacking anything" (James 1:3 – 4).

Oh, sweet sisters, this truth should be the cry of our souls instead of Satan's lie that "it's not fair." Our taste buds make such empty claims to satisfy us, but only persevering with God will make us truly full, complete, not lacking anything.

Press on, sisters. Press on.

Personal Reflections

1. Recall the last special occasion or celebration you attended. What foods were present that you knew probably weren't good choices for you? If you ate them, how much of your decision was influenced by telling yourself this was a special situation and deserved an exception? If you passed them by, did you nevertheless resent your choice because it didn't seem fair?

2. "Temptation doesn't take kindly to being starved" (page 101). Have you experienced what it's like to starve temptation in any area of your life? What happened? How did it make you feel? For example, did you feel peaceful and empowered or like a tug-of-war was raging in your heart?

3. Lysa says she recognizes that having a pity party is a clue she is relying on her own strength rather than God's strength. What clues you into the fact that you are relying on your own strength in your battles with food?

4. Have you ever felt as if issues with food and weight were God's unfair curse on you or wished your struggle could be with something other than food? In what ways might your struggle be beneficial or even a blessing?

5. When facing a moment of indecision about food, Lysa recommends thinking beyond the moment by saying, "This feels good now, but how will I feel about this in the morning?" Thinking back to the last time you ate something you later regretted, do you believe asking yourself this question would have changed your decision? Why or why not?

6. "Compromise built upon compromise equals failure....
[P]romise upon promise creates empowerment" (page 104).
Some decisions about food may seem inconsequential in the
moment, but even small decisions can have a big impact over
time. In which direction are your small decisions about food
leading—toward failure or empowerment?

7. "The struggle to say no may be painful in the moment, but it
is working out something magnificent within us" (page 104).
What is the magnificent thing you hope God might do in you
through your struggles to say no?

Stinkin', Rotten, Horrible, No Good Day

I just don't have it in me to stick with this healthy eating thing," Amy quipped in utter exhaustion. Life had been spinning out of control in every area— troubled finances, a stressful marriage, struggling family members, and on and on. Because she couldn't control much about her life, Amy felt she could no longer limit her food choices. Food was her numbing drug of choice.

When her bills ran high and her cash flow short, ice cream from her freezer would do the trick.

When marriage stresses overwhelmed her emotions and there seemed to be no end to the conflicts, leftover Halloween candy was an easy thing to sneak by the fistfuls.

When another bad report came about her dad's cancer, French fries and a chocolate shake soothed her raw nerves.

When her house seemed messy, dusty, and chaotic, she escaped to the local coffee shop where a grande, extra-whip, triple-shot, white chocolate mocha made life feel smooth and sweet.

When her struggling child brought home another failing grade, she decided it was a great day to head off to the Mexican restaurant down the street where they could both get lost in huge bowls of chips and salsa.

Forty-seven pounds later she sat crying on her bathroom floor. "What am I doing to myself?" she sobbed. She'd been carrying the weight of the world on her shoulders and now everything was compounded by all the weight she'd added to her body.

Tears streamed down her cheeks as she crawled into bed and glanced at the photo on her bedside table. There she was, nearly fifty pounds ago, smiling and hugging her husband. Where had that happy girl gone? Where had that happy couple gone? And when was the last time they'd even touched?

A deep knot of insecurity twisted in her gut at the thought of her husband seeing her now. More tears. More desperation. More hopelessness. And the only thing she wanted in that moment was the bag of Goldfish crackers and the half carton of Oreos sitting in her pantry.

Goldfish? Oreos? My life is falling apart and my body is expanding more and more by the minute and all I can think about right now is Goldfish and Oreos? It is a stinkin', rotten, horrible, no good day. Right now would be a really good time for the earth to implode and swallow me up into a dark hole. Or for Jesus to come back. And speaking of Jesus, what an utter disappointment I must be.

Amy felt a dark depression slipping over her like heavy blanket. A blanket so bleak and black she thought it might strangle the life out of her.

> *Isn't it just like Satan to make us think we have to have something to comfort us, only to be haunted by the consequences of this comfort later?*

Ever been there? I have. Isn't it just like Satan to make us think we have to have something to comfort us, fill us, satisfy us, only to be haunted by the consequences of this comfort later?

Getting a Handle on Food during Hard Times

In the previous chapter, we talked about being tempted during times of celebration. But I think it worth chatting about being tempted to overeat and make poor choices during times of struggle as well—those times when you just don't have it in you to deny yourself unhealthy foods. Life is already denying you so much. For heaven's sake, everything you want seems out of reach but these cookies are right here. And you want them. And they will taste good. And no one has the right to say you can't have them. So there.

Obviously, I've been around this mountain a time or two or twenty-seven. But I love what my friend Ruth Graham says about traveling around the same mountain for far too long.

> Either we can be victimized and become victims, or we can be victimized and rise above it. Often it is easier to play the victim than take off our masks and ask for help. We get comfortable with our victim status. It becomes our identity and is hard to give up. The Israelites often played the victim card, and I love what God finally tells them, "You have circled this mountain long enough. Now turn north" (Deuteronomy 2:3 [NASB]).
>
> Turn north! It's time to move on! Self-pity, fear, pride, and negativity paralyze us. Taking off our masks takes courage, but if we don't do it, we will remain in our victim status and end up stunted.[6]

Or in this case, overweight and unhealthy, further compounding our feelings of being victimized by our circumstances. So, what can we do when we don't have the energy or the fortitude or the desire to eat healthy?

This is an important thing to tackle because if there is one thing I know about life, it will be dotted with hard times. So, we've got to get a plan to realistically handle them. We've got to get a plan to refuse to head south with our healthy eating plan and keep our compasses set to true north. I love God's command to "turn north" and stop circling this mountain. And, as Ruth states, an important part of turning north is taking off our masks and asking for help.

For me, this starts with taking off my mask before the Lord and asking Him to help me find fulfillment in my relationship with Him.

You have circled this mountain long enough. Now turn north.

This is hard sometimes. Taking off my mask means I have to admit that there's a problem, and I really don't want to do that. Admitting I have a problem will likely require that I make changes, and changes are hard. Food gives such an instant rush and tangible good feeling. It's so much easier to figure out how to get the short-term high of a cookie than it is to get a heart filled up and satisfied with God. I can drive to the store and fill my arms with any kind of cookies I want. But wrapping my arms around getting "filled up" with God during a particularly empty feeling day doesn't seem as tangible or immediate.

I know I should pray. But I'll be honest again and admit that I'm done with praying fake, plastic prayers when I'm struggling. Rote prayers I've repeated thousands of times just won't cut it when unhealthy snack options are calling to me from the pantry and my resolve has worn as thin as a tissue. I've been known to pray as I'm stuffing myself full, "God, thank you for this food. Take it to the nourishment of my body and please change the molecular structure of these Goldfish into that of carrot sticks."

Since I hardly think that's a sign of taking off my mask, getting honest with God, and heading north, I have to have another prayer strategy. I have to find a way to be filled up and satisfied with God's love. And a few years ago, I found exactly what I needed — prayers where I don't speak at all.

Prayers Where I Don't Speak at All

I had been going through some stinkin', rotten, horrible, no good days and was at the absolute end of knowing what to pray. I'd slipped into a habit of praying circumstance-oriented prayers where I'd list out every problem and ask God to please fix them. I even made suggestions for solutions in case my input could be useful. But nothing changed. Except my waist line and the amount of chocolate life suddenly required.

In a huff one day, I sat down to pray and had absolutely no words. None. I sat there staring blankly. I had no suggestions. I had no solutions. I had nothing but quiet tears and some chocolate smeared across my upper lip. Eventually, God broke through my worn-out heart. A thought rushed through my mind and caught me off guard, *I know you want Me to change your circumstances, Lysa. But, right now I want to focus on changing you. Even perfect circumstances won't satisfy you like letting Me change the way you think.*

I didn't necessarily like what I heard during this first time of silently sitting with the Lord, but at least I felt I was connecting with God. I hadn't felt that in a long time. And so, to keep that connection, I started making it a habit to sit quietly before the Lord.

Sometimes I cried. Sometimes I sat with a bad attitude. Sometimes I sat with a heart so heavy I wasn't sure I'd be able to carry on much longer. But as I sat, I pictured God sitting there with me. He was there already and I eventually sensed that. I experienced what the apostle Paul taught when he wrote, "In the same way, the Spirit helps us in our weakness. We do not know what we ought to pray for, but the Spirit himself intercedes for us with groans that words cannot express" (Romans 8:26).

As I sat in silence, the Spirit interceded with perfect prayers on my behalf. I didn't have to figure out *what* to pray or *how* to pray about this situation that seemed so consuming. I just had to be still and sit with the Lord. And during those sitting times, I started to discern changes I needed to make in response to my circumstances —none of which included using food for comfort.

I think a lot of us try to get filled up with things or people. In *Becoming More Than a Good Bible Study Girl*, I talked about how I walked around for years with a little heart-shaped cup, holding it out to other people and things trying to find fulfillment. Some of us hold out our heart-shaped cup to food. Others demand that husbands love us in ways that right our wrongs and fill up our insecurities. Sometimes we expect our kids to be successful so we look good and have our worth validated by their accomplishments. Or we overspend our budget on an outfit we just have to have.

Whatever it is, if we are really going to stop circling the mountain and head north toward lasting changes, we have to empty ourselves of the lie that other people or things can ever fill our hearts to the full. Then we have to deliberately and intentionally fill up on God's truths and stand secure in His love.

The more I fill myself up with the truths of God's love, the less I find myself pulling out that little heart-shaped cup. I have to mentally replace the lies using some of my favorite verses to remind myself of just how filling God's love really is. Here are some examples of how I do that:

Old Lie: I need these Oreos. They will fill me up with a chocolate high and taste so good.

New Truth: The thought that these Oreos will fill me is a lie. They will taste good for just the few minutes it will take to eat them. Then that hollow feeling of guilt will rush in as soon as the chocolate high dissipates. Do I want to eat right now because I need nourishment or because I'm feeling empty emotionally or spiritually? If I truly need a snack right now, I am capable of choosing a healthier option.

Favorite Verse: "And I pray that you, being rooted and established in love, may have power, together with all the saints, to grasp how wide and long and high and deep is the love of Christ, and to know this love that surpasses knowledge—that you may be filled to the measure of all the fullness of God." (Ephesians 3:17–19)

Old Lie: I am such a failure with this healthy eating thing. Why sacrifice this instant gratification now when I know eventually I'll just go back to my old habits anyhow?

New Truth: I am not a failure. I am a lavishly loved child of God. Part of my right as a child of God is to operate in a power beyond myself. The Holy Spirit is God's gift to me so it is possible for me to use the self-control I've been given.

Favorite Verse: "How great is the love the Father has lavished on us, that we should be called children of God! And that is what we are!" (1 John 3:1)

Old Lie: God seems so far away and French fries are right around the corner at the drive-thru.

New Truth: French fries don't love me. And the only lasting thing I get from them is the cholesterol and cellulite they inevitably leave behind, which will just compound my frustration. God's love is here in this moment and in many more to come. His love is true and carries with it only positive residual effects.

Favorite Verse: "But from everlasting to everlasting the LORD's love is with those who fear him." (Psalm 103:17)

This is just a start of replacing the lies and rationalizations with the truths of God's love. I encourage you to write out some old lies and new truths on your own. The process of stripping away old lies is hard and can produce raw feelings. That's why it's so crucial to have truths with which to replace them.

When I posted a small portion of these thoughts on my blog, I received some very raw and honest responses. But one especially grabbed my heart because Kim is seeing how beneficial replacing old lies with truths can be. She said:

French fries don't love me. The only lasting things they give me are cholesterol and cellulite.

What you wrote today was clearly from God for me to hear. I have lived the last twenty-eight of my forty years of life trying to get someone to fill me, love me, need me, make me worthy, all in an effort to compensate for the abuse—mental, emotional, and physical—and then complete abandonment of my father, brother, and paternal side of the family.

Food? Honey, let me tell you that 350 pounds later, I am finally getting that food is not a substitute for God's love. It's almost destroyed me. My marriage is in shambles; we separated this past Friday. Our five-year-old daughter is stressed, acting out, you name it, she is there.

This is *not* the life I want. This is *not* the life I plan to continue to lead. If ever God spoke to me, what you wrote today went right to the heart of the matter. Thank you for being faithful. Thank You, God Almighty, for loving me. I am one step into a future that has real hope—hope that God fulfills.

I pray we are all with Kim on this journey of replacing lies, embracing truth, and learning that food was never meant to fulfill the deepest places of our hearts reserved for God alone. Not on the good days. Not on the bad days. And not even on the stinkin', rotten, horrible no good days. God says, "See, I have placed before you an open door that no one can shut" (Revelation 3:8). May it be that we walk through that door, head north, and never look back.

Personal Reflections

1. Recall a recent stressful experience that tempted you to overeat or make poor food choices. What specific feelings did the experience elicit (for example: anger, embarrassment, tension, sadness, anxiety, grief)? Whether you resisted or gave into temptation, how were your emotions impacted as a result?

2. When you experience problems or difficult seasons in life, are you more likely to put on a mask and pretend everything is okay or to take off your mask and ask for help? How has this tendency impacted your ability to resist food temptations at such times?

3. Discovering how to pray without words helped Lysa to feel like she was connecting with God, something she hadn't felt in a long time (page 113). Have you ever prayed this way, simply spending time with God in silence and allowing the Holy Spirit to intercede on your behalf (Romans 8:26)? Does this idea intrigue you or scare you?

4. Lysa demonstrates how she replaces old lies about food with new truths about God's love (page 114). In the course of a regular day, what old lies about food make it difficult for you to resist temptation? Do hard times make these lies harder to resist? Drawing on what the Bible teaches about God's love in Ephesians 3:17 – 19, 1 John 3:1, and Psalm 103:17, what new truths might you use to replace your old lies?

5. "See, I have placed before you an open door that no one can shut" (Revelation 3:8). If God were to speak these words directly to you about your struggles with food, what do you hope you would see and experience on the other side of the door?

The Curse of
the Skinny Jeans

In the last chapter, we talked about sticking to our healthy eating plan during times when rotten days try to throw us off-kilter. Once I reached my goal weight, I thought I'd never really have those off-kilter days again. I mean, really, what could possibly trouble me if I could fit into my skinny (thought I would never wear them again) jeans?

Boy was I wrong.

It should have been a week of absolute rejoicing. I'd reached a major mile marker in my healthy eating journey — results. Tangible, amazing, thought-I-might-never-see-this-day results. My skinny jeans fit. I was not only able to get them pulled all the way up and buttoned, but I could still breathe! Oh, yes ma'am, I could breathe and move and even sit down without the fear of busting the seams.

Have you ever known this kind of crazy? Like most women, I had kept this pair of skinny jeans in my closet. They had made it through many, many closet purges. All of my other jeans from a size I hadn't seen in quite a while had long since been bagged up and taken to Goodwill. But this particular pair of jeans had been spared as a symbol of a promise I'd made to myself to one day lose the weight — again.

Every now and then I got the jeans out, crossed every possible finger and toe, and attempted to defy the odds by putting them on. I pulled and tugged and lay down on the floor to try and stretch this denim that must have shrunk in the dryer. I knew in my head it was not a case of laundry gone bad, but my heart was living in denial. With my refusal to make changes in my unhealthy eating habits, the possibility of me ever wearing those jeans was nothing but wishful thinking.

Until now.

As I slipped the jeans on and buttoned them with ease, my smile could not be contained. I danced around my bedroom throwing my hands in the air. Victory, victory, sweet, sweet victory! I felt like I could take on the world. Until, just hours later, my world made me cry.

A hurtful email. A disrespectful attitude from one of my kids. A missed appointment. A condemning feeling of irresponsibility. A messy house. A stressful situation at work. An unexpected bill. A dinner that was left basically untouched by my family. A spider in my tub.

I found myself getting snappy with my family, irritated with the sender of the email, on edge about the mess and stress, frustrated by that bill, and mad that no one liked my dinner. So, by the time I found the spider in my one spot of relaxation, my emotions unraveled and frayed.

How could I feel this way? I was wearing my skinny jeans, for heaven's sake. And I always thought, *If only I could put on those skinny jeans, my whole world would fall into place and put a permanent smile on my face.*

Yet, here I was, just hours later, falling prey to the same topsy-turvy stuff I used to think wouldn't bother me if only I were smaller. This is the curse of the skinny jeans. My body size is not tied to my happy. If my happy was missing when I was larger, it will still be missing when I get smaller.

Tying My Happy to the Wrong Things

Tying my happy to the wrong things is partially what caused my weight gain in the first place. There were too many experiences I enjoyed primarily because of the food that was attached to them. The movies were tied to popcorn. A birthday party was tied to cake. A ballgame was tied to a hotdog. School parties were tied to cookies. A morning meeting was tied to gourmet coffee. Getting gas was tied to snack crackers and a soda. Watching TV was tied to chips. A summer outing was tied to ice cream. A winter outing was tied to hot chocolate.

Tying my happy to food, skinny jeans, or anything else sets me up for failure. Not to mention that once I slip on those skinny jeans, my elation is quickly marred by the fear of gaining back the weight.

And I'm not the only one who knows the curse of the skinny jeans. I once read an interesting commentary on this issue by Oprah. And while Oprah and I don't agree on some things, we can agree that tying our happy to the wrong things sets us up for failure every time. She said, "I grew up believing that people with money didn't have problems. Or certainly none that money couldn't solve. Then in 1986, my show went national. It changed the trajectory of my life. . . . In 1992, I won another Emmy for Best Talk Show Host." She went on to say she'd prayed she wouldn't win because she was so embarrassed by her weight at the time. "And 237 pounds was the heaviest I'd ever been. I had journals filled with prayers to God to help me conquer my weight demon."[7]

Tying my happy to food, skinny jeans, or anything else sets me up for failure.

Oprah had everything she ever thought would make her happy. Money. Fame. Recognition. Success beyond many of our wildest dreams. And at one point, thanks to a crazy liquid diet, she dropped down to 145 pounds and wore skinny jeans. I remember being a teenager at the time, glued to that day's show when the skinniest Oprah I'd ever seen revealed her new body.

But none of that brought her lasting happiness. It may have brought moments of temporary thrills, but waiting for her at home were those journals filled with prayers asking God to help her. Even on the day she wore those skinny jeans.

Remain

I can totally relate. I have to learn to attach my happy to the only eternal stability there is and remain there. Oh, the prayers I have prayed over and over and over for God to help me, stabilize me, and tie my happy only to Him. It's called learning to remain. Isaiah 55:8–12 illustrates so beautifully exactly what I'm talking about:

> "For my thoughts are not your thoughts, neither are your ways my ways," declares the LORD.
>
> "As the heavens are higher than the earth, so are my ways higher than your ways and my thoughts than your thoughts.
>
> As the rain and the snow come down from heaven, and do not return to it without watering the earth and making it bud and flourish, so that it yields seed for the sower and bread for the eater, so is my word that goes out from my mouth: It will not return to me empty, but will accomplish what I desire and achieve the purpose for which I sent it.
>
> You will go out in joy and be led forth in peace."

Did you catch how satisfying God's words are? They are compared to water that makes the earth bud and flourish. That's why Jesus' words in John 15 are so crucial for us to apply if we're ever going to have lasting joy ... whether or not we are wearing our skinny jeans.

Here's how Jesus describes it:

As the Father has loved me, so I have loved you. Now remain in my love. If you obey my commands, you will remain in my love, just as I have obeyed my Father's commands and remain in his love. I have told you this so that my joy may be in you and that your joy may be complete. My command is this: Love each other as I have loved you. (John 15:9 – 12)

I'll admit, I've read these verses many times while nodding and saying, "Yeah, yeah, I've read this before. That's nice."

But just recently, something new jumped out at me and begged me to park my brain in the truths I'd only been skimming. We are taught to remain in God's love so that we won't tie our happy to anything but God. So that our joy will be complete.

Complete. As in not lacking anything. Complete. As in filled up to the brink with joy no matter if we are wearing our skinny jeans or not. Complete. As in satisfied with a fullness we can't get any other way. Can you imagine how beautiful it would be to live as a complete person?

Incomplete people are difficult, demanding, and always in pursuit of that next thing that will surely fill them. Incomplete people think that putting on their skinny jeans will right all their wrongs and fill up all their insecurities. Incomplete people quickly find out their skinny jeans adjust nothing in their lives except the number on the tag no one else sees.

Incomplete people are desperate for others to notice their diet progress, but quickly realize compliments don't assure connection or intimacy. They

Incomplete people think that putting on their skinny jeans will right all their wrongs and fill up all their insecurities.

are not more liked or accepted or welcomed in. And even if they are being liked based on a smaller jeans size, what an awfully shallow place to be.

The bad news is, we're all incomplete people. The good news is, Jesus loves incomplete people. And He wants us to know we can have complete joy by being secure enough in His love to reach out and love other incomplete people.

Afternoon Acts of Kindness

I'll admit, loving incomplete people doesn't seem like the obvious path to joy. And it doesn't seem like an obvious topic to be covered in a book on getting healthy and keeping our skinny jeans in proper perspective. But stick with me here, you might be surprised.

Just the other day I was pondering some of those distressing emails I mentioned earlier, and I reached the conclusion that incomplete people are a trigger that make me want to eat. They are complicated and sensitive and messy in their reactions. They have the potential to drain my resolve and make me grumpy.

What if I could be courageous enough to act and react like a complete person — a Jesus girl who has His joy in her, sustaining her, and directing her?

The last thing I want to do when a person throws their incompleteness in my direction is love them. I want to grab a bag of Cheetos and rationalize how much a treat is certainly in order right now. Then I want to sit on my couch and tell the air around me how much I love Cheetos and how much I dislike incomplete people.

But what if I dared in that moment to think differently? What if I could be courageous enough to act and react like a complete person — a Jesus girl who has His joy in her, sustaining her, and directing her? Instead of looking at this incomplete person's offense, what if I could see the hurt that surely must be behind their messy reaction?

I pause. I don't reach for the Cheetos. I don't react harshly out of my own incompleteness. I don't wallow in my thoughts of how unfair and unkind this other person is. And I choose to love instead. Quietly, taking out a piece of stationery and responding with words of grace. Or crafting an email with a message of compassion.

Better yet, what if I were to do this every afternoon, even when I haven't had a run-in with an incomplete person but am just simply craving things I shouldn't eat? I've been trying this out lately and I love it. Afternoon acts of kindness are yet another unexpected but beautiful result of letting Jesus direct my healthy eating pursuits.

Each day I've been asking Jesus who in my life needs words of encouragement and He always puts someone on my heart. So, instead of filling my afternoons with thoughts of frustration toward others or tempting thoughts about food, I am filling my afternoons with His thoughts of love toward others. And this is a great place to be no matter if I'm wearing my skinny jeans or not.

After all, remember the ultimate goal of this journey isn't about making me a smaller sized person but rather making me crave Jesus and His truths as the ultimate filler of my heart. We are to remain in this healthy perspective. Let His thoughts be our thoughts. Remain. Let His ways be our ways. Remain. Let His truths go to the depths of our hearts and produce good things in our lives. Remain. Approach this world full of fellow incomplete people with the joy of Jesus. Remain. And see our skinny jeans as a fun reward, nothing more. Remain. And be led forth in peace because I've kept my happy tied only to Jesus. Remain.

Personal Reflections

1. What fantasies do you have about what life would be like if you were at your ideal weight? Do you imagine everything in your life would somehow be better — your relationships would improve, your confidence would soar, your problems would fall away, you'd be respected, admired, obeyed? Why do you think

your weight has so much power to influence your outlook on life?

2. Movies and popcorn, parties and cake, ballgames and hotdogs, meetings and coffee, TV and chips. What activities do you enjoy in part or primarily because of the food attached to them? Which activities might lose all attraction for you if food weren't part of the experience?

3. "We are taught to remain in God's love so that we won't tie our happy to anything but God" (page 123). To what other things besides God have you tried to tie your happy? What was the result? Do you think it's possible for you to feel full of joy even if you're not where you want to be with your weight? Why or why not?

4. "[Incomplete people] are complicated and sensitive and messy in their reactions" (page 124). Who are the incomplete people in your life? Are these people triggers that make you want to eat? Are there ways in which you might be an incomplete person in someone else's life? For others as well as yourself, are you able to look beyond the incompleteness to the hurt that may be behind the messy reactions? What do you see?

5. Compassion for incomplete people — including ourselves — translates into acts of kindness. When you think of the incomplete people in your life, especially those who may be eating triggers, how might a compassionate act of kindness change how you feel about that person? How might it change how you feel about yourself and your own incompleteness?

13

Overindulgence

I didn't quite know what to think as my pastor walked up to the podium with a bottle of wine and proceeded to pour a glass. Just about everyone shifted in their seats while he let the shock of the moment settle in. Really settle in.

Seeing a bottle of wine on center stage in a Bible Belt church just doesn't happen. Ever. We drink grape juice for communion.

He then asked us to stand for a reading of God's Word, which was the passage in John 2 where Jesus turns water into wine. The point of his sermon was to clear away some cultural debris — taboos about drinking wine — so that we could see what the Bible really says and accept it as part of the larger truth of God's Word. It was a mighty fine sermon full of verses that dispelled the myths that the wine Jesus filled the water jars with that day was unfermented, watered down grape juice. It was wine. Wine that Jesus Himself, who never sinned, drank.

Of course, he handled this teaching very delicately. Those who are underage or who have issues with alcohol and can't have a glass of wine without being irresponsible should avoid it altogether. He also touched on not being a stumbling block to those who struggle. But again, whether or not to have a glass of wine with dinner was not the point of the sermon; the point was to know what the Bible says about issues we face every day and to apply those Scriptures to our lives appropriately.

Then he shifted gears and turned his attention to food.

Now this really was an historic church-going day. Seeing wine in the sanctuary was shocking enough, but never have I heard a preacher man talk about gluttony in church. Never. And his point was brilliant. How can we stand and wag our fingers in the direction of alcohol only to walk into the church-wide covered dish buffet and stuff ourselves sick with fried, covered-and-smothered, grossly caloric delights that buckle our paper plates and cause our stomachs to cry for antacids?

Overindulgence is overindulgence. And limitless indulgence in food always has consequences—it compromises our health, diminishes energy to pursue our calling, and affects the way we feel about

> *Limitless*
> *indulgence in*
> *food always has*
> *consequences.*

ourselves, just to name a few. It's at this point that we have to admit our issues with food aren't just little things that require us to wear a larger-than-ideal dress size. Eating in excess is a sin. The Bible calls it gluttony, which is defined in the dictionary as "excess in drinking or eating."[8]

The biblical teaching about excess drinking and eating is clear. "Do not join those who drink too much wine or gorge themselves on meat, for drunkards and gluttons become poor, and drowsiness clothes them in rags" (Proverbs 23:20–21). Here's another: "He who keeps the law is a discerning son, but a companion of gluttons disgraces his father" (Proverbs 28:7).

I doubt we'll ever see either of these verses on the "Suggested Memory Verse for the Week" Sunday school bulletin board. They're hard verses. This is a hard topic.

I imagine at this point you are wondering if we really need to go there with this gluttony thing. It's not exactly the most girlfriend-fun topic that makes you say, "Preach on, sister. I'm loving this encouragement!"

And I doubt I'll be packing out any arenas if I ever decide to advertise a weekend conference on gluttony. But we have to go there and let me tell you why. On the surface it appears that all we're talking about is food and the amount we consume. In reality, there is a more serious issue at the root of gluttony. Overstuffing ourselves with food or drinking until we get drunk or getting wrapped up in the affections of an adulterous relationship are all desperate attempts to silence the cries of a hungry soul.

A Soul Longing to Be Filled

A starved soul is like the vacuum cleaner my mother used when I was a child. It had a long metal tube that ravenously sucked up anything and everything set before it. It sucked up dust bunnies with the same furor as a $10 bill. I know that one from experience.

Our souls have the same ravenous intensity as my mother's vacuum cleaner; that's how God created us — with a longing to be filled. It's a longing God instilled to draw us into deep intimacy with Him. The psalmist expresses this longing as an intense thirst: "As the deer pants for streams of water, so my soul pants for you, O God. My soul thirsts for God, for the living God. When can I go and meet with God?" (Psalm 42:1–2). "I spread out my hands to you; my soul thirsts for you like a parched land" (Psalm 143:6).

If we fail to understand how to fill our souls with spiritual nourishment, we will be triggered to numb our longings with temporary physical pleasures.

Indeed, our souls are thirsty and ravenous vacuums. If we fail to understand how to fill our souls with spiritual nourishment, we will forever be triggered to numb our longings with other temporary physical pleasures. When those pleasures are food, the resulting behavior is what we often hear referred to as "emotional eating." But this issue is bigger than emotions; it's really about spiritual deprivation.

My boyfriend breaks up with me. I want a tub of ice cream.

That big business deal falls through. I'll take the super-sized fries, please.

I don't feel pretty. I need some chocolate to soothe and delight me.

My kids are driving me crazy. I deserve a piece of cake. I deserve three pieces.

I hate cleaning my house. When I'm done I'll treat myself to as many chips as I want.

It's my birthday and I don't really think anyone cares. I'll just eat my way into happiness or numbness. Same difference, right?

I hardly think it ironic that I'm struggling even as I write these words. There's a situation in my life that has wormed its way straight to the most vulnerable of places in my heart. This situation has made me feel hurt and rejected. Years ago a little crack in my strong resolve was created by the extreme rejection of my biological father. And while I've found amazing victory in understanding I'm no longer a child of a broken parent but rather a child of God, revisiting rejection is never fun.

I've realized when the desire for treats is triggered by difficult emotions, it's not really a desire for treats—it's a thinly veiled attempt at self-medication.

We'll talk more about emotional emptiness in the next chapter. For now, let's focus on the triggers that come on hard days ... days when part of me says, "Today is a day you deserve treats, Lysa. Just one day of eating whatever you want and as much as you want." But just because I've reached my goal weight in this journey and operate in a good place most of the time does not mean I can drop my guard and fall back into old habits. It's such a slippery slope.

I'm not saying we shouldn't allow ourselves the occasional treat. We should. But I've realized when the desire for treats is triggered by difficult emotions, it's not really a desire for treats—it's a thinly veiled attempt at self-medication. And self-medicating with food even once triggers vicious cycles I must avoid.

It's also important to note that not all gluttony is caused by emotional responses. Sometimes it's just an overindulgence because we lack the self-control to say enough is enough. And it breaks my heart how much people in the church simply turn their heads the other way when it comes to this issue.

So, What Are We to Do?

A few years ago, the words *portion control* took on new meaning as I studied the book of Exodus and noted the curious emotional response God's people had after Moses led them out of slavery in Egypt. They'd just seen God do miracle after miracle to help them escape their captors, but they panicked when it came to food.

> In the desert the whole community grumbled against Moses and Aaron. The Israelites said to them, "If only we had died by the LORD's hand in Egypt! There we sat around pots of meat and ate all the food we wanted, but you have brought us out into this desert to starve this entire assembly to death."
>
> Then the LORD said to Moses, "I will rain down bread from heaven for you. The people are to go out each day and gather enough for that day. In this way I will test them and see whether they will follow my instructions." (Exodus 16:2–4)

In other words, God planned to use the Israelites' food issues to teach them the valuable lesson of daily dependence on Him. Don't you love how applicable this is to us? Ancient biblical stories have taught me that history certainly has a way of repeating itself, so I'd be wise to pay attention. Because these recently freed Israelites continued to grumble against God and turn their hearts from Him, God took them on a forty-year detour. Instead of heading straight to the Promised Land of freedom, they had to wander in the desert for forty years while they learned how to truly depend on God.

I don't know about you, but I don't want to spend the next forty years of my life learning this lesson. I want to stop grumbling about my weight, apply this valuable training about God-dependence and portion control, and keep walking toward the victory that can be mine. So, how did God teach His ancient people to depend on Him daily?

Each day the Israelites were to ask God for their portion of food. Then God would rain down exactly what they needed for nourishment. It was called *manna*, which I imagine was something like little, sweet, potato flakes. The Israelites were to go out each day and collect just enough manna for that one day.

They were never to gather up extra and build big storehouses of manna supplies where they could set up drive-thru windows for McManna Happy Meals. No, God wanted them to take only their portion for one day. The next day they would come to Him and again receive their daily portion. The only exception to this was the day before Sabbath when they could gather a double portion so they wouldn't have to work on the holy day. It was a process intended to put them in the habit of dependence on God, and only God, each day.

We would do well to apply this same process to our struggles. Each day God can be the perfect portion of everything we need — every longing we have, every desperate desire our souls cry out for. God will be our portion. With this in mind, let's revisit a few of the emotional struggles we noted earlier that can often trigger a gluttonous response.

My boyfriend breaks up with me. Instead of grabbing a tub of ice cream, I ask God to be my daily portion of companionship in this lonely time. "God, I hate this rejection and hurt. Sometimes I feel like the loneliness is going to swallow me alive. I can't deal with this on my own. Will You be my portion of healing and companionship just for this day?"

That big business deal falls through. Instead of ordering the pasta dish drowning in cream sauce at lunch, I ask God to be my portion of strength to order the grilled chicken salad. I pray, "God, I so desperately want comfort right now and that pasta with cream sauce seems like it would be so comforting. It hurts so much that I've lost this deal. Feeling like a failure makes me want to say, 'Who cares,' and eat whatever. Will You be my portion of comfort and strength and success in this moment?"

My kids are driving me crazy. Instead of wolfing down three pieces of chocolate cake, I pray, "God, I so desperately want to be a patient mom. I don't know if I can be a patient mom the rest of my life. But with Your portion of strength I can rely on You in this moment and not try to medicate my shortcomings with food."

I keep asking God to be my daily portion.

Whatever the situation, I keep asking God to be my daily portion — of companionship, provision, patience — over and over. And one day I will find victory over those things instead of just looking back over a pile of tears and cake crumbs. Here's a biblical promise we can rely on:

> Because of the LORD's great love we are not consumed, for his compassions never fail. They are new every morning; great is your faithfulness. I say to myself, "The LORD is my *portion*; therefore I will wait for him." (Lamentations 3:22 – 24, emphasis added)

Grasping the truth that God is our portion has the potential to transform more than just our eating habits; it can transform our responses to every aspect of our lives. Practicing God's portion control was crucial for the spiritual development of the Israelites and it's crucial for our spiritual development as well. God doesn't mince words about His expectations or His promises:

> You shall have no foreign god among you; you shall not bow down to an alien god. I am the LORD your God, who brought you up out of Egypt. Open wide your mouth and I will fill it. (Psalm 81:9 – 10)

Whether we are talking about food, wine, sex, shopping, or anything else with which we try to fill ourselves, nothing in this world can ever fill us like God's portion. Nothing else can truly satisfy. Nothing else is unfailing and absolute. And I don't say all this with a quirky little smile hoping it works. I shout it from the depths of my soul because I know it works, "for he satisfies the thirsty and fills the hungry with good things" (Psalm 107:9).

Personal Reflections

1. What are the unspoken truths about food at your church or in your circle of Christian friends? In terms of how they eat and relate to food, is your Christian community an asset or a liability to your healthy eating goals?

2. Gluttony of any kind — food, alcohol, drugs, sex — could be described as a desperate attempt to silence the cries of a hungry soul. Have you ever thought of overeating in this way, as an attempt to silence your hungry soul? How might this perspective help you gain new insights about your battles with food?

3. If your soul is like a ravenous vacuum cleaner, what kinds of things has it sucked up over the years in its longing to be filled?

4. Lysa uses the Exodus story to demonstrate how God taught His people to depend on Him by giving them just what they needed each day (pages 131 – 132). In what ways might this story be an encouragement to you? Are you in the habit of depending on God for what you need each day — to be your daily portion of companionship, provision, strength? What "manna" do you long for most from God?

5. Have there been times in your life when you struggled because you didn't have what you needed? How might these experiences of deprivation impact your ability to trust that God can give you what you need each day to deal with food?

6. "For he satisfies the thirsty and fills the hungry with good things" (Psalm 107:9). How do you respond to this promise? If you could ask God for one good thing that would help you to feel a deep and soul-filling satisfaction, what would it be?

Emotional Emptiness

Sometimes people struggle with food because they eat too much of the wrong kinds of foods and they consume more calories than their body needs. When their energy output is less than their food intake, the excess is stored as fat.

One pound of fat is equivalent to 3,500 calories, which makes gaining or losing weight a pretty straightforward mathematical equation. In order to lose weight, we need to burn more calories than we consume so our stored fat is burned off as fuel.

And while all this is as true for me as the next person, there are things that make the prospect of losing weight a little more complicated for me than just the numbers. Somewhere behind all the math, a less measurable force is at work within me. It takes the form of emptiness or lack. As I trace my fingers back across the timeline of my life, I can remember times when spiritual and emotional emptiness left me vulnerable. The shape of my lack was the absence of a biological father. It was as if someone held up my family photo and excised his form from our lives with laser-like precision.

There we were — my mom, my sister, and me — with this misshapen family and a hole that extended way deeper than an excised photograph. All of him was gone. His face that should have looked upon his children with adoration. His arms that should have worked to provide for us. His feet that I should have been allowed to stand on while he danced me around the den. His mind that should have shared wisdom about why pet hamsters die and why boys sometimes break girls' hearts. His heart that should have been filled with compassion and desire to shelter us from the storms that scared us so.

Everyone has hurts from their past.

He took with him so much more than he ever could have imagined. Those few suitcases and plastic crates didn't just contain boxers, ties, old trophies, and dusty books. Somewhere in between his Old Spice and office files were shattered pieces of a little girl's heart.

Now I'm not a big fan of pointing to hurts from my childhood and saying, "All my issues can be linked back to what other people did to me. Let me cut open my hurts and wallow in all that leaks out." At some point, I came to the realization that everyone has hurts from their past. And everyone has the choice to either let those past hurts continue to haunt and damage them or to allow forgiveness to pave the way for us to be more compassionate toward others.

But the reality of my dad's abandonment created some unhealthy habits that continued to linger in my life. Emptiness has a way of demanding to be filled. And when I couldn't figure out how to fill what my heart was lacking, my stomach was more than willing to offer a few suggestions. Food became a comfort I could turn on and off like a faucet. It was easy. It was filling. It was available. It became a pattern. And somehow, each time my heart felt a little empty, my stomach picked up on the cues and suggested I feed it instead.

When I decided to get healthy with my eating, I started by praying a very simple prayer, "Unsettle me." I'll talk more about this prayer in chapter 17, but I mention it now because during my unsettling process I became aware of how emotional emptiness is a trigger for my eating. Much of this emotional emptiness stemmed back to that little girl coming home from school and being told, "Your daddy's gone." That one event was so huge, so draining, that it caused me to fill my mind with only negative memories of my dad. In my mind, he never loved me at all.

And you know what? Maybe he didn't. But parking my mind only on negative thoughts about my dad left such a sadness in my heart. Though I've been touched by Jesus and my soul filled with God's good perspective and healing truths, there was still this very human part of me that felt so incredibly sad when I thought about what never was with my daddy.

Sometimes I could brush off this sadness with a little sigh and recitation of who I am in Christ. But other times it made me angry. And defensive. And hungry. And deeply unsatisfied.

I honestly never thought anything but sadness was ever possible with my dad. I'd reached out to him with a few phone calls and letters over the years, but no miraculous restoration ever took place. No beautiful ending where he suddenly knocks on my door and says, "I'm sorry." No note that finally made its way to me after years of being lost that read, "I have always loved you." No beautiful crescendo of music as the story of my life with Dad suddenly reads, "Happily ever after."

None of that. Just unresolved hurt and this nagging feeling that his absence was partially due to me not being what he wished I would have been. That's a heavy weight for a little girl to carry. That's a heavy weight even for us big girls.

Then one day God surprised me in the most unusual way. As I said, I'd been praying for God to unsettle me and make me aware of all those places I'd resigned were impossible to change. And while my dad still made no effort to connect with me, a sweet memory of him changed my dark perspective.

Last winter Art and I traveled to Vermont where I woke up one morning to stare at what an overnight snowstorm brought us. I had never seen such snow in all my life. But what really caught my attention were the gigantic icicles hanging from the roof line. They were glorious.

As I stared out at them, suddenly a memory of my dad flashed across the screen of my mind.

I grew up in Florida, which meant no snow ever. But I remember praying for snow. Praying like a revival preacher at a tent meeting, I tell you. If ever there could be snow in Florida, surely a passionate little girl's prayers could open up those heavenly storehouses where all snowflakes are kept.

One night the temperatures dropped surprisingly low and the weatherman called for a freeze, which was a rare thing in our area. How tragic there was no precipitation. It was the one night that snow might have been possible.

It broke my little snowbunny heart.

But the next morning I awoke to the most amazing sight. There were icicles everywhere. Gleaming, dripping, hanging, light-reflecting, glorious icicles were all over the trees in our backyard.

It was magical.

We were the only house on the block with this grand winter display.

Because I was the only girl whose daddy thought to intentionally put sprinklers out on the one night it froze.

I don't know where this memory had been hiding for too many years. But what a gift. Somewhere in the deep, mysterious, broken places of my dad's heart, there was an inkling of love.

And while this certainly doesn't solve all the complications of being abandoned by my dad, it gives me a healthy thought to dwell on where he's concerned — one of those good thoughts the Bible tells us to think about: "Whatever is true, whatever is noble, whatever is right, whatever is pure, whatever is lovely, whatever is admirable—if anything is excellent or praiseworthy—think about such things" (Philippians 4:8). I like to call this "parking my mind in a better spot."

It's so easy to park our minds in bad spots. To dwell and rehash and wish things were different. But to think on hard things keeps us in hard spots and only serves to deepen our feelings of emotional emptiness. This is where pity parties are held and we all know pity parties demand an abundance of high-calorie delights, eaten and eaten some more. But pity parties are a cruel way to entertain, for they leave behind a deeper emptiness than we started with in the first place.

To think on hard things keeps us in hard spots and only serves to deepen our feelings of emotional emptiness.

And there I would sit with a guilt-ridden mind, a bloated stomach, an empty heart, and a soul full of anger that my dad was continuing to hurt me even all these years later.

But this icicle memory gave me a new place to park. A place where I could pursue truth rather than chocolate. A place where lovely could be something besides nachos in the Taco Bell drive-thru. And excellent could be my victorious response of turning to habits such as prayer, reading Scriptures, and exercising away my stress rather than snacking away my emptiness.

What about you? Do you have something from your past that causes emotional emptiness? As a first step toward healing, can you think of one thing good from this past situation? Or maybe something good that has happened despite the pain from the event? If not, ask God to give you some good place to park your mind with this draining issue from your past. Then, try walking through the following exercise based on Philippians 4:8. Here's how I did this with the emptiness I felt about my dad:

Whatever is true: My dad was broken. Only broken daddies

leave their children. This isn't a reflection of me. It's simply a sad reflection of the choices he made. But it's also true that he had to reach past his brokenness that one night to set up the sprinklers for his little girl. And as small as this one act is, it was an act of love.

Whatever is noble: I don't have to live as the child of a broken parent the rest of my life. I can live as a daughter of the King of Kings. Who not only wants me but has promised to never, ever leave me. As a matter of fact, the Bible promises me, "The Lord is near" (Philippians 4:5). And the Lord was near the night of sprinklers. Though my dad professed to be an atheist, I'm convinced Jesus broke through his tough exterior that night and was near to him. Even if he didn't receive Jesus, my dad was near enough one night to see how beautiful love can be. I hope Dad remembers.

Whatever is right: Everything right and good in this life has God's touch on it. It makes me smile to think there must have been two sets of fingerprints on that old, rusty, yellow sprinkler that night. My biological daddy carried it, set it up, and turned it on. But my heavenly Daddy made sure the sprinkler was positioned just right to form icicles that froze the trees and warmed my heart.

Whatever is pure: God has set eternity in the heart of every human being (Ecclesiastes 3:11). So, even with all the darkness that seemed to surround my dad, some pure light of selflessness broke through and gave evidence of something good working within him. Warmth on a cold night. Purity in the midst of messy sin, broken hearts, and tainted lives.

Whatever is lovely: God can take ugly and build lovely from it. After all, He's called the Potter, right? From the dust of the earth, He formed human beings. He healed a blind man by rubbing mud on the ailing man's eyes. That is a lovely quality about God. That lovely spilled over and helped my dad think of icicles. Really lovely icicles. And in the midst of a backyard that never saw games of catch, a treehouse, or father-daughter talks, there was once a glorious display of lovely that only we had.

Whatever is admirable, excellent, or praiseworthy: I wouldn't say my dad was admirable, excellent, or praiseworthy. But then again, maybe I should. Maybe like the icicles there are other memories long forgotten and covered over by the darkness of his cruel departure. In the end, my Lord has taken those shattered pieces of my heart and removed them from the boxes my dad carried away that awful day.

Piece by piece, God has created a mosaic in my heart—one of restoration, healing, and compassion. I am the person I am today in part because of the hurt of being left behind by my dad. I wouldn't have chosen that piece of my mosaic, but how good of God to place right beside the hurt a clear piece of glass shaped like those warm icicles from so long ago. A memory I can think on. A memory that fills me better than any piece of chocolate cake or nacho chips. A memory that is true, noble, right, pure, lovely, admirable, excellent, and praiseworthy. And filling.

So, back to that mathematical equation from earlier. I'm no math whiz, but I do remember there being these things called polynomials. Polynomials are algebraic expressions that include real numbers and variables. That's the way my food issues are—they contain real numbers and variables. I suspect yours do as well. And while we must pay attention to the real numbers by eating less and moving more, we would do well to consider the variables in our lives as well.

> *We must deal with our triggers. We must identify our places of emotional emptiness and admit how futile it is to try and fill those places with food.*

We must deal with our triggers. We must identify our places of emotional emptiness and admit how futile it is to try to fill those places with food. I realize what I've written here is but a first step in this process. Often these issues are big and complicated and a bit like peeling back the layers of an onion. Just when you think you've tackled a piece of it, you realize there are many layers yet to go.

If you need more help, be honest with yourself and seek out a good Christian counselor. Often churches can recommend counselors in your area that base their advice on biblical truths. I wouldn't be where I'm at today without seasons I spent getting counselors to speak truth into my life.

But for today, finding a gentle memory in the midst of a mess is a good start. A really good start. One that is lovely, and true, and worth looking for.

So, Dad, should you ever stumble upon these words I pray you remember the night of the icicle wonder. For it is a common thread of hope that ties two very distant hearts together.

And that makes me smile.

Personal Reflections

1. "Each time my heart felt a little empty, my stomach picked up on the cues and suggested I feed it instead" (page 138). Do you feel a similar connection between feelings of emotional emptiness and physical hunger? Do you feel you are able to distinguish between physical hunger and emotionally triggered hunger, or does it all feel the same to you?

2. Lysa describes how she used the phrases of Philippians 4:8 to park her mind in a better spot about the painful relationship with her father. Using the phrases below and Lysa's example as a guide (pages 141–143), invite God to give you a better place to park your mind about a painful experience from your own past.

   • Whatever is true ...

   • Whatever is noble ...

   • Whatever is right ...

   • Whatever is pure ...

   • Whatever is lovely ...

   • Whatever is admirable, excellent, or praiseworthy ...

3. A mosaic is a work of art made up of hundreds or thousands of tiny, broken pieces of glass or ceramic tile. Lysa describes how God is making a mosaic of restoration and healing in her heart, gathering up her broken pieces and making them into something beautiful. Can you imagine God doing something like this in your heart? If God used the broken pieces of your life to make a beautiful image, what do you hope it would look like?

15

The Demon in the Chips Poster

In the past three chapters we've been talking about replacing the old go-to scripts of rationalization with truth. Maybe I'm the only crazy dieter full of rationalizations, but there's one more we must address and it's this: "If no one sees you, then the calories don't count."

I know this makes absolutely no logical sense. But, girlfriend, sneaking when no one else is looking will absolutely kill a healthy eating plan. So, when I hear this rationalization playing out in my head, I don't try to replace it with another go-to script. Instead, I flee. I have to remove myself from the vicinity of the temptation.

Remember, this isn't just a battle in the physical and mental realm. This battle is spiritual as well. Satan wants us to sneak things in secret. Things hidden and done in secret clues the father of darkness into our weaknesses and opens the door for him to assault us with targeted schemes. That's why the apostle Paul wrote, "Be strong in the Lord and in his mighty power. Put on the full armor of God so that you can take your stand against the devil's schemes" (Ephesians 6:10 – 11).

This isn't just a battle in the physical and mental realm. This battle is spiritual as well. Satan wants us to sneak things in secret.

Here's how pastor and author Chip Ingram characterizes Satan's schemes:

They are orchestrated in order to tempt us, deceive us, draw us away from God, fill our hearts with half-truths and untruths, and lure us into pursuing good things in the wrong way, at the wrong time, or with the wrong person. The English word *strategies* is derived from the Greek word Paul uses that is translated "schemes." That means our temptations are not random. The false perspectives we encounter do not come at us haphazardly. The lies we hear, the conflicts we have with others, the cravings that consume us when we are at our weakest points — they are all part of a plan to make us casualties in the invisible war. They are organized, below-the-belt assaults designed to neutralize the very people God has filled with his awesome power.[9]

Did you catch what Chip included in his list of Satan's specific schemes? *Cravings that consume us when we are at our weakest points.* Yet we must remember we hold a power greater than any craving we face. Just the other night I faced one of my fiercest battles with this.

I had a busy day and decided to grab take-out at one of my favorite restaurants on my way home. I ordered grilled fish and steamed broccoli. Pleased with my choice and my self-discipline, I proceeded to the pickup area. That's when the assault started.

A giant poster of the best chips and salsa you've ever seen was hanging over the take-out register. The girl behind the counter was trying to ask if I needed plastic ware and to confirm my order was correct.

Inside my brain a weak-willed woman started screaming, "No, my order is not correct. I need chips. Lots and lots of those chips. I need that salt. I want that crunch. With every fiber in my being I want to shove this fish and broccoli back across the counter and demand, "CHIPS!"

It was like those chips were dancing in front of me and singing the words from that '80s tune, "Don't you want me baby … don't you want me, ohhhhhh oh?"

I wanted to start reciting that old script in my head that would justify me right into a chips frenzy: "You've had such a hard day. You've been good for so long. Who would ever know? And if no one else knows, the calories don't really count, right? Plus, it's just one order of chips and salsa. Everything else you ordered is so healthy. One order of chips can't possibly be that bad. Just do it this time and then be good for the next couple of days."

I wanted to play that script. I wanted the chips. But something else was tugging at my mind. Truth.

Lots of Scriptures we've already covered came to mind. They sprang forward and started doing battle with the old script trying to lead me astray. I could feel the tension. Literally, as I stood there taking way too long to answer the girl about whether or not I needed a plastic fork, truth and lies were fighting for my attention. That's when it occurred to me. I held the power to determine who would win.

I held the power.

Not the chips.

And the power was to acknowledge that I'm not yet at a place where I can handle just a few chips. My brokenness cannot support that kind of freedom. Therefore, I had to flee. I had to remove myself from the source of temptation and I had to do it immediately.

I had to remove myself from the source of temptation and I had to do it immediately.

My hollow stare suddenly became an unwavering look of determination. "Yes, I do need a fork with this fish and broccoli." I can picture the girl rolling her eyes as she bent down to get my fork wondering what kind of fruit loop has to think for such an inappropriate amount of time about whether or not she needs a fork.

But I wasn't focused on her or her quizzical expression. Instead, I forced myself to focus on walking out that door. As I drove home, one verse kept coming to mind: "They gave in to their craving . . . they put God to the test" (Psalm 106:14). In my mind I repeated it over and over until my healthy dinner and I were far away from the demon disguised as a chips-and-salsa poster.

By the time I got home and filled myself with the healthy fish and steamed broccoli, I realized I had no desire for chips and salsa. None. I was satisfied with my healthy choices. So, what made the difference?

Let's take a closer look at that verse in Psalms: "In the desert they gave in to their craving; in the wasteland they put God to the test." The desert is a place of deprivation. In a deprived state we are much more likely to give in to things we shouldn't. I was really hungry when I walked into that restaurant, which made those chips and salsa look even better than usual. I was in a weakened state and faced with something that could instantly and easily fill me. That's what I call a danger zone.

Inside a danger zone the lies and rationalizations of the enemy sing so sweetly. Alluring sights and smells coupled with salivating taste buds specifically arranged by the enemy for my destruction. Without trying to be overly dramatic, this is the exact point at which I must start reciting truth, pack up my fish and broccoli, and flee. Flee, I tell you. Literally and deliberately flee.

I had to stop thinking about what I *shouldn't* have and park my mind on thoughts of being thankful for what I *could* have. I could have delicious grilled fish and steamed broccoli. Food that is healthy and beneficial for giving my body strength. We must embrace the boundaries of the healthy eating plan we choose. We must see them as parameters that define our freedom with things like grilled fish and broccoli, not as horrible restrictions keeping us from chips and salsa. And we must affirm these boundaries as gifts from a God who cares about our health, not restrictive fences meant to keep us from enjoying life. Vulnerable, broken taste buds can't handle certain kinds of freedom. So, boundaries keep us safe, not restricted.

I had to stop thinking about what I shouldn't have and park my mind on thoughts of being thankful for what I could have.

I learned this through our sweet little dog, Chelsea. She is not the brightest bulb in the lamp around cars driving down our long driveway. Though she has plenty of room to run and play inside our fenced-in yard, she is obsessed with trying to attack the tires crunching against our gravel drive whenever someone drives on our property. As a result, she had her second unfortunate encounter with a moving vehicle about the same time I started my healthy eating plan.

I wept like a baby when I saw her. But, other than a broken front leg, a severely scraped up back leg, and a nose with half the flesh missing, she fared okay. Mercy.

The vet informed us that in order for her leg to properly heal, we'd have to keep her calm for three weeks. I asked if he could give her some nerve pills and throw a few in for me too. I am not beyond borrowing some of my dog's medicine if it keeps me from going crazy. Because that is exactly where I thought I might be headed, having just been handed the assignment to keep my dog still for three weeks. It would be a challenge to keep Chelsea still for three minutes. But three weeks?

Well, two weeks into the healing journey all that stillness got the best of sweet Chelsea in the middle of the night. She decided she would punish me with a fit of whining, crying, and banging my closed bathroom door. She wanted out and she wanted out now. She wanted to run and chase some unsuspecting night creature. The temptation was too strong and she was sick of sacrificing her freedom.

To be honest, I wanted her to be able to run and chase a night creature too. Oh, did I ever. But my love for this dog would not permit me to allow her to harm herself. Her brokenness couldn't handle that kind of freedom.

Not yet.

And as I tossed and turned in the wee hours of the morning, the truth behind that statement about Chelsea's brokenness struck me as quite applicable to myself as well. My brokenness couldn't handle freedom with food outside the boundaries of my plan.

Not yet.

Eventually, I will be able to add some things back into my diet in small quantities.

But, not yet.

My brokenness with food runs deep. I am a girl who begged God to send a magic fat-burning pill down from heaven because I just could not find the willpower to fight this battle on my own. Y'all, I prayed for a fat-burning pill. No, I take that back. I begged for a fat-burning pill. With tears in my eyes.

Boundaries keep us safe, not restricted.

Not my finest godly girl moment.

So, because my brokenness with food runs deep, my new healthy habits have to have time to run even deeper. Here are some of the healthy boundaries I have set to ensure success on my healthy eating adventure. For your convenience I've also included these at the end of the book (pages 215–216) for a quick reference guide after you've finished reading. I highly recommend reading through these often. They've really proven to be helpful for me to stay in a good place with my healthy habits.

- God has given me power over my food choices. I hold the power — not the food. So, if I'm not supposed to eat it, I won't put it in my mouth.

- I was made for more than being stuck in a vicious cycle of defeat. I am not made to be a victim of my poor choices. I was made to be a victorious child of God.

- When I am struggling and considering a compromise, I will force myself to think past this moment and ask myself, "How will I feel about this choice tomorrow morning?"

- If I am in a situation where the temptation is overwhelming, I will have to choose to either remove the temptation or remove myself from the situation.

- When I'm invited to a party or another special occasion rolls around, I can find ways to celebrate that don't involve blowing my healthy eating plan.

- Struggling with my weight isn't God's mean curse for me. Being overweight is an outside indication that internal changes are needed for my body to function properly and for me to feel well.

- I have these boundaries in place not for restriction but to define the parameters of my freedom. My brokenness can't handle more freedom than this right now. And I'm good with that.

This battle is hard. Really hard. Whether you are staring at a church covered-dish table heavy laden with all things breaded, fried, and smothered in cheese, or you are standing in a restaurant staring up at a chips-and-salsa poster, it can feel like a war is being waged in your head. So, I pray these boundaries help you like they've helped me.

It breaks my heart that so many of God's girls feel powerless in this struggle. Let's band together, get honest, grab hold of the truths that will set us free, and do something about it. Victory is possible, sisters, not by figuring out how to make this an easy process, but by choosing—over and over and over and over again—the absolute power available through God's truth.

Personal Reflections

1. Congratulations! You've been chosen to participate in the latest reality TV show. How much would your eating change if you knew that dozens of tiny hidden cameras were strategically placed throughout your home, car, and workplace, recording everything you ate and broadcasting it live on a local cable channel? Would your eating change a little or a lot if you knew that nothing you ate was secret?

2. As Lysa was modifying her eating, she had to flee some temptations because her brokenness could not handle certain freedoms. What areas of brokenness in your life aren't yet capable of handling freedoms? How do you typically respond to temptations in these areas?

3. When it comes to boundaries with food, it's important to focus on what we *can* have rather than what we *can't* have. When you think of what you can have right now, for what three to five foods are you most grateful? How might focusing on these foods keep you from dwelling on the foods you can't have right now?

4. Lysa describes seven healthy boundaries that are helping her on her eating adventure. For each of the boundaries listed below, place an X on the continuum to indicate whether the boundary feels more like a punishing restriction or a hedge of safety for you.

God has given me power over my food choices. I hold the power — not the food. So, if I'm not supposed to eat it, I won't put it in my mouth.

This boundary feels like a punishing restriction.   This boundary feels like a hedge of safety.

I was made for more than being stuck in a vicious cycle of defeat. I am not made to be a victim of my poor choices. I was made to be a victorious child of God.

This boundary feels like a punishing restriction.

This boundary feels like a hedge of safety.

When I am struggling and considering a compromise, I will force myself to think past this moment and ask myself, "How will I feel about this choice tomorrow morning?"

This boundary feels like a punishing restriction.

This boundary feels like a hedge of safety.

When faced with an overwhelming temptation, I will either remove the temptation or remove myself from the situation.

This boundary feels like a punishing restriction.

This boundary feels like a hedge of safety.

When I'm invited to a party or another special occasion rolls around, I can find ways to celebrate that don't involve blowing my healthy eating plan.

This boundary feels like a punishing restriction.

This boundary feels like a hedge of safety.

Struggling with my weight isn't God's mean curse for me. Being overweight is an outside indication that internal changes are needed for my body to function properly and for me to feel well.

This boundary feels like a punishing restriction.

This boundary feels like a hedge of safety.

I have these boundaries in place not for restriction but to define the parameters of my freedom. My brokenness can't handle more freedom than this right now. And I'm good with that.

This boundary feels like a punishing restriction.

This boundary feels like a hedge of safety.

Take a moment to review your responses. What do they reveal about how you view boundaries? Which boundary feels most like a restriction? Is this something you've struggled with before? What boundary feels most like safety? How might you lean into this boundary to give you strength and confidence with the boundaries that might be harder for you to keep?

16

Why Diets Don't Work

I have issues with infomercials. I do. They suck me in and make me a believer in slick slogans and paid actors giving fake testimonials. I've ordered everything from grout cleaner to face powder, magic cleaning cloths to veggie steamers, and a meat griller that practically promised to grab the meat out of my fridge and cook it with absolutely no effort on my part.

However, no infomercials grab my attention quite like diet ones. With big promises and little sacrifice, you too can be a size smaller by this afternoon. And while everything in my brain screams, "It's a scam!" something in my heart says, "But maybe this one is the sure thing."

Maybe this one really will make me feel so full I can eat three peas and half a chicken breast and be satisfied until dinner. Maybe this one really will block every bit of fat I consume from being absorbed in my body, thus allowing me to eat, eat, eat, without gaining, gaining, gaining.

In the end though, my rational mind helps my wishful-thinking taste buds put the phone down, slip my credit card back into my wallet, and make peace with reality. There are no quick fixes.

But I have to hand it to them. These infomercial people are smart because they've figured out a way to tap into the harsh reality of why diets fail. We get tired of sacrificing and our self-effort wears thin.

I know what that feels like.

I'm Not on a Diet

Just today I was walking through the Chicago airport with some apple slices in my purse for a snack. I was perfectly happy with my apples until I walked past a smell that grabbed me by the collar, got right in my face, and said, "Don't you know how much happier I can make you?" A shop called Nuts on Clark had just made a fresh batch of caramel popcorn.

I love caramel popcorn. And I could easily rationalize purchasing some. I can't get this brand in North Carolina. It could be my special Chicago treat. How much could it really hurt to consume one bag of caramel popcorn? Lots of other people were getting it.

Really, I could have gotten the popcorn, eaten a few handfuls and saved the rest for my kids, and been perfectly fine with my little diet cheat. The problem is, I'm not on a diet.

Diets don't work for me. I seem to be able to sacrifice for a season and then I get tired of sacrificing. I hit my goal weight and then slowly slip back into old habits. The weight creeps back on and I feel like a failure. Like I said, diets don't work for me.

I'm not on a diet. I'm on a journey with Jesus.

So, I'm not on a diet. I'm on a journey with Jesus to learn the fine art of self-discipline for the purpose of holiness. And today I'd decided ahead of time, I would have apples for a snack, not caramel popcorn.

Deciding ahead of time what I will and will not eat is a crucial part of this journey. I also try to plan my meals right after breakfast when I'm feeling full and satisfied. Deciding in advance keeps my thinking and planning rational and on track. The absolute worst time for me to decide what I'm going to eat is when I've waited until I'm depleted and feeling very hungry. At that point my body is screaming for something quick, and usually quick things come in a full variety of unhealthy temptations.

Here's a biblical perspective on temptation: "If you think you are standing strong, be careful not to fall. The temptations in your life are no different from what others experience. And God is faithful. He will not allow the temptation to be more than you can stand. When you are tempted, he will show you a way out so that you can endure" (1 Corinthians 10:12–13, NLT). The way out the Lord provides for me is deciding in advance what I will and will not have each day.

Deciding ahead of time what I will and will not eat is crucial.

Now, here's another interesting part to all this. Keeping these verses in context, verse 14 of this same chapter goes on to say, "Therefore, my dear friends, flee from idolatry" (NIV). Oh, how this verse points a finger straight at my personal issues with food and says, "This is exactly why this has to be a spiritual journey and not a temporary diet."

Expecting anything outside the will of God to satisfy us is idolatry. Nutrition, which is food's intended purpose, means consuming proper portions of healthy choices that enable our bodies to function properly. Idolatry, in the case of food, means the consumption of ill-sized portions and unhealthy choices because we feel like we deserve it or need it to feel better.

Now, hear me on this. We aren't to flee food. We need food. But we are to flee the control food can have over our lives. If we flee from the pattern of idolizing food and stop depending on food to make us feel emotionally better, we will be able to more clearly see the way out God promises to provide when we are tempted.

Two Elephants in the Room

At this point in the chapter, as we're talking about those feelings of deserving certain foods or needing a treat to get by, I think it quite appropriate to address two elephants in the room.

Elephant 1: **"It's my party, and I'll eat cake if I want to.**
Don't tell me I have to give up all treats for all time."

I'm not saying we have to give up all treats for all time. When I was working toward getting to a healthy weight, I did give up all sugar and starchy carbs for a season. When I reached my goal weight, I added some things back to my eating but did so very carefully. Note the words *some* and *carefully*.

We aren't to flee food. But we are to flee the control food can have over our lives.

I'm not saying that enjoying these occasional treats is wrong. Now that I'm at my goal weight, if I were to decide in advance to have popcorn at the movies, then I would have a small popcorn (no butter). For the next several days I would be more careful with my healthy eating regimen and pass on adding in any treats.

I can't go back to my old habits of thinking I deserved a special treat every day. The realities of diet failure speak loudly and clearly that returning to old habits will cause the weight I've lost to return as well.

A study reported in the *Journal of the American Medical Association* compared a two-year weight loss among 65 men and 358 women of various weights (but all considered "obese"), randomly assigned to two different diets. After the first year, the average weight loss was about 9.5 pounds on one program, versus just under 3 pounds on self-help. But at the two-year mark, the average participant had regained some of the weight lost, so the net loss was 6.4 pounds for the one versus half a pound for the other. Here are some comments from the research team:

> Although [we] drew the conclusion that the first program was "more effective" than the other, it doesn't take a degree in statistics to realize that the diet program failed to produce a significant and lasting weight loss. This is the first real clinical proof

of what we have been saying all along: diets are not effective as a long-term strategy for weight loss, in part because people regain most or all of the weight they lose. If the scientists had followed their subjects for another three years, we are certain that the weight regain would have been even more dramatic.[10]

Though this journey isn't all about weight loss, weight is a measurable indicator of whether or not we're making healthy choices. These diet failure statistics prove what I've experienced in previous weight loss attempts—prolonged success is really difficult. Which leads me to the second elephant in the room.

Elephant 2: "I don't think this sounds like a spiritual journey. I think this sounds like a legalistic approach to eating."

Please hear my heart on this. I am not writing this book to set forth legalistic rules about eating. I am writing this book as an invitation to consider the freedom found when we bring one of our most basic of needs—food—before the Lord and allow Him to guide and guard us in this area.

We *do* need a healthy eating plan, which some will refer to as a diet. But we must have a depth of restraint that can only come from making this a spiritual growth journey. Putting all of our hope in religious adherence to a human-designed diet can create a false sense of prideful self-effort, harsh treatment of the body and, in the end, usually failure.

The apostle Paul addressed this issue when he wrote his letter to the Colossians:

> Since you died with Christ to the basic principles of this world, why, as though you still belonged to it, do you submit to its rules: "Do not handle! Do not taste! Do not touch!"? These are all destined to perish with use, because they are based on human commands and teachings. Such regulations indeed have

an appearance of wisdom, with their self-imposed worship, their false humility and their harsh treatment of the body, but they lack any value in restraining sensual indulgence. (Colossians 2:20–23)

In commenting on these verses, pastor Ray Stedman writes:

A legalist looks at life and says, "Everything is wrong unless you can prove by the Bible that it is right. Therefore, we must have nothing to do with anything that the Bible does not say is right." That reduces life to a very narrow range of activity. But the biblical Christian looks at life and says, "Everything is right! God has given us a world to enjoy and live in. Everything is right, unless the Bible specifically says it is wrong." Some things are wrong; they are harmful and dangerous. Adultery is always wrong. So is fornication. Sexual promiscuity is wrong. Lying and stealing are wrong. These things are never right. But there is so much that is left open to us. If we are willing to obey God in the areas that he designates as harmful and dangerous, then we have the rest of life to enter into company with a Savior who loves us, and who guides and guards us in our walk with him.[11]

I especially love that last sentence, *If we are willing to obey God in the areas that he designates as harmful and dangerous*—and we learned in the previous chapter that gluttonous behaviors are not just dangerous; they are sinful—*then we have the rest of life to enter into company with a Savior who loves us, and who guides and guards us in our walk with him.*

Entering into company with my Savior is indeed what I must do for this healthy-eating, spiritual journey to be successful and long-lasting. It's the component that all previous diets I've tried were missing. Even the medical community is starting to pick up on the crucial role of making any weight loss and healthy eating journey a spiritual commitment.

Dr. Floyd Chilton, a physiologist who teaches at Wake Forest University School of Medicine, puts it this way:

> Your willpower is in constant battle with your genes and your calorie-excessive environment. Often your best efforts are no match for your genes and environment which is why so many diets fail so miserably.... Willpower alone is not enough to bring about this change; start by realizing that you cannot do this alone. If you are a person of faith, use that connection to help you change.[12]

I couldn't agree more, Dr. Chilton. God created us and told us to be faithful with the bodies we've been given. The Holy Spirit empowers us to make lasting change. And Jesus lovingly guides and guards us as we walk with Him, moment by moment, choice by choice, day by day.

And that's a plan with a promise no infomercial can ever offer!

Personal Reflections

1. Have you ever been lured in by the promises of an infomercial or fad diet? What was it about the diet that appealed to you most? Did it guarantee quick results? Promise you could eat whatever you wanted and still lose weight? What about it made you think, *Maybe, just maybe this one is a sure thing*? How did you feel when it didn't deliver as promised or you gained back the weight you'd lost?

2. Lysa describes her experiences of diets as sacrificing for a season and then regaining the weight when she gets tired of sacrificing. Instead, she says she is now "on a journey with Jesus to learn the fine art of self-discipline for the purpose of holiness" (page 158). What do you think about this distinction between diets and a journey with Jesus? How might your decisions about food and healthy eating change if you could really see them as part of a spiritual journey rather than a diet? Is this an idea that feels possible for you or unrealistic? Why?

3. "God is faithful; he will not let you be tempted beyond what you can bear. But when you are tempted, he will also provide a way out so that you can stand up under it" (1 Corinthians 10:13). This is a promise with which many of us who grew up in church are very familiar, maybe too familiar. Do you believe, really believe way down deep, that this promise applies to you and your temptations with food? For Lysa, God's "way out" is to plan in advance what she will eat. How hard is it for you to look for a way out when temptation catches you off guard?

4. "Idolatry, in the case of food, means the consumption of ill-sized portions and unhealthy choices because we feel like we deserve it or need it to feel better" (page 159). Do you agree with this definition? If so, when was the last time you committed idolatry with food? What prompted you to do so? If not, do you believe it is possible to make an idol out of food? Why or why not?

5. There are two elephants in the room when Lysa talks about feelings of deserving certain foods or needing a treat to get by:

   • *Elephant 1:* "It's my party and I'll eat cake if I want to. Don't tell me I have to give up all treats for all time."

   • *Elephant 2:* "I don't think this sounds like a spiritual journey. I think this sounds like a legalistic approach to eating."

   With which elephant do you most resonate? Do you feel you can eat treats as you usually do and still make healthy choices? Do you resist the idea that your battle with food can become a liberating spiritual journey? What past experiences inform your views?

The Very Next
Choice We Make

Whenever anyone hears of my weight loss and healthy eating plan, they immediately ask two questions:

"How did you do it?"

"Is this something you can sustain?"

Maybe throughout this journey, you've had people asking you these same questions.

I imagine that what people are really asking is something like this: *If I were to start on this healthy eating plan, what would I have to sacrifice? And, if I make that sacrifice for a season, can I eventually go back to eating whatever I want without regaining the weight?*

Both are very valid questions. Questions that I've asked myself about every healthy eating plan I've ever tried. Sacrificing for a season is not fun, but it is doable. It introduces us to the benefits of discipline and feels achievable for a short while.

But sacrificing until we no longer desire what has been given up? Well, that just takes discipline to a whole new level. A level where some will take a brief vacation but very few put down permanent roots.

I recently had a fascinating discussion about discipline with three pastors. The question was thrown out, "Is discipline really sustainable?" One chuckled as he stuffed a second yeast roll in his mouth and said, "Obviously, not for me."

The second leaned back in his chair and expressed his doubt as well.

The third piped in with an absolute yes and gave biblical support for his emphatic answer.

I never got to give my answer that day. We had a tight schedule and our conversation turned to other matters. But if I had been able to give my answer, it would have been this: no and yes.

No, I do not believe in our own strength we can sustain a level of discipline that requires real sacrifice for a long period of time.

However, my answer is yes when you factor in a crucial spiritual truth. Making the connection between my daily disciplines with food and my desire to pursue holiness is crucial. Holiness doesn't just deal with my spiritual life; it very much deals with my physical life as well.

It is good for God's people to be put in a place of longing so they feel a slight desperation. Only then can we be empty enough and open enough to discover the holiness we were made for. When we are stuffed full of other things and never allow ourselves to be in a place of longing, we don't recognize the deeper spiritual battle going on.

We need to be empty enough and open enough to discover the holiness we were made for.

Satan wants to keep us distracted by chasing one temporary filling after another. God wants us to step back and let the emptying process have its way until we start desiring a holier approach to life. The gap between our frail discipline and God's available strength is bridged with nothing but a simple choice on our part to pursue this holiness.

Moment by moment we have the choice to live in our own strength and risk failure or to reach across the gap and grab hold of God's unwavering strength. And the beautiful thing is, the more dependent we become on God's strength, the less enamored we are with other choices.

I was challenged by the third pastor's emphatic response that sustained discipline is possible. He said, "God tells us to be holy. So, be holy. He wouldn't have said it if it weren't possible."

Like I said before, "Making the connection between my daily disciplines with food and my desire to pursue holiness is crucial. Holiness doesn't just deal with my spiritual life; it very much deals with my physical life as well." This is a truth the apostle Paul affirmed when he wrote, "Since we have these promises, dear friends, let us purify ourselves from everything that contaminates body and spirit, perfecting holiness out of reverence for God" (2 Corinthians 7:1).

Holiness means to be set apart for a noble use. The very next choice we make isn't really about whether or not to eat chips, cookies, or French fries smothered in chili and processed cheese. It's about whether we are going to stay away from those things that are not beneficial for what we are created to be. We are "taught, with regard to [our] former way of life, to put off [our] old self, which is being corrupted by its deceitful desires; to be made new in the attitude of [our] minds; and to put on the new self, created to be like God in true righteousness and holiness" (Ephesians 4:22–24).

We were created to be God's representatives as we live out loud the message of God in our daily lives. But I'll be honest, the last thing I feel like doing when I'm living in a defeated state with my food issues is to reach out to other people. I don't want to "be made new in the attitude of my mind," nor do I want to "put on my new self created to be like God in true righteousness and holiness."

I want to cry.

I want to withdraw.

I want to be jealous that others don't have my issues.

I want to be mad at God for giving me this metabolism.

I want my very next choice to be high in calories, fried in fat, and drizzled with something that makes my taste buds sing.

I want victory, but I feel so weak.

This hardly sounds like someone who has conquered her food issues, right? The reality is, even when we stand on the scale and see our goal weight staring back at us, we're always just one choice away from reversing all the progress we've made. I'm not saying victory isn't possible. But victory isn't a place we arrive at and then relax. Victory is when we pick something healthy over something not beneficial for us. And we maintain our victories with each next choice.

Here's a biblical perspective from the apostle Paul: "I put this in human terms because you are weak in your natural selves. Just as you used to offer the parts of your body in slavery to impurity and to ever-increasing wickedness, so now offer them in slavery to righteousness leading to holiness" (Romans 6:19). You see, the very next choice we make isn't really about the food and the weight and the negative feelings we carry around when we're choosing poorly. It's about whether or not we're positioning ourselves to live the kind of God-honoring lives in which, by God's strength, sustained discipline is possible.

So, how does one tap into God's strength? Certainly prayer. Definitely reading the Bible. We've talked quite a bit about both of those throughout this book. But there's another part to it. Getting to a place where our lack of strength disgusts us.

This place is found at the bottom of our excuses and rationalizations. It's found when our efforts fail time and time again. It's found in the humility of this admission: "I need God to unsettle me."

I got to this place on New Year's Day 2009 as I flippantly thought about my new year's resolutions. Like a vast majority of people, the holiday pounds were making my clothes pull and protest. Again. And these were my big clothes. So many years I had vowed to do better and here I was again, defeated. I didn't want to write a cheesy resolutions list that would wind up in the bottom of my purse torn, tattered, and eventually used to wrap a chewed piece of gum.

But I did want to do something. I needed to do something. So, instead of a list, I wrote out my heart's cry in a blog post titled "Unsettle Me."

Unsettle me.

These are the two words rattling about in my brain today. I almost wish it were a more glamorous prayer. Surely more eloquent words could be found for what I'm feeling led to pursue during this new year.

But these are the words and this is the prayer for my 2009.

The funny thing is, I've spent my whole existence trying to find a place to settle down. People to settle down with. And a spirit about me worthy of all this settled down-ness.

All of this is good. A contented heart, thankful for its blessings is a good way to settle.

But there are areas of my life that have also settled in ways that mock my desires to be a godly woman. Compromises, if you will.

Attitudes that I've wrapped in the lie, "Well, that's just how I am. And if that's all the bad that's in me, I'm doing pretty good."

I dare you, dear soul of mine, to notice the stark evidence of a spirit that is tainted and a heart that must be placed under the microscope of God's Word.

Yes, indeed, unsettle me, Lord.

Unearth that remnant of unforgiveness.

Shake loose that justification for compromise.

Reveal that broken shard of pride.

Expose that tendency to distrust.

Unsettle me in the best kind of way. For when I allow Your touch to reach the deepest parts of me — dark and dingy and hidden away too long — suddenly, a fresh wind of life twists and twirls and dances through my soul.

I can delight in forgiveness and love more deeply.

I can discover a discipline that lies just beyond what I'm capable of and grab hold of God's strength to bridge the gap.

I can recognize the beauty of humility and crave the intimacy with God it unleashes.

I can rest assured though harsh winds blow, I will be held.

Goodbye to my remnants, my rationalizations, shards, and tendencies. This is not who I am nor who I was created to be.

Goodbye to shallow love, sharp words, self-pity, and suspicious fears. I am an unsettled woman who no longer wishes to take part in your distractions or destructions.

Welcome deeper love, new possibilities, unleashed intimacy, and the certainty I am held.

Welcome my unsettled heart.

Welcome 2009.

I had to decide if I wanted to live in a place of sustained discipline and make the choice that I wouldn't see it as a curse. Rather, I'd see it as something good, something I could embrace. One good choice later, I tasted the empowerment of possibility and I started reaching forward from there.

Robin is in the process of reaching forward from a place of waffling with her discipline. I love what she wrote in an email to me:

After reading your post a few days ago, it encouraged me to go back to not eating sweets. I did it for three months hoping I would be delivered in that short time. But you know it took me a lifetime to get this way, so who am I to put a time limit on God? Your email, coupled with what my fifteen-year-old son said to me a few weeks ago, just kept ringing in my ear. He said something like, if you have diabetes ... you don't stop taking your medicine just because you feel better. So why would I go back to eating unhealthy just because I feel better? I have a long way to go, but I know this is going to be a life-changing deliverance from my emotional eating. I will have to deal with the problem instead of snacking away at it.

I love the honest admission at the end of Robin's email, where she says she has to deal with the problem rather than "snacking away at it." Remember at the beginning of this book we talked about cravings? Even though we've made significant progress during our journey, we'll still be surprised by cravings and the desire to snack away our issues.

Crave means to long for; want greatly; desire eagerly. Pursuing holiness means God is the only One we should long for; want greatly; desire eagerly. The only One worthy of worship.

Throughout my journey I've been doing a lot of reading in Psalms, Scriptures that beautifully illustrate why worshipping God is what we were made to do. I'm not sure I've ever studied this book with such hunger to better understand my Lord. The pages of Psalms in my Bible are now heavy-laden with underlines, notes, journaled thoughts, exclamation points, arrows, and aha moments. One of those moments came as I read Psalm 78:

God did miracles — verse 12.
He divided the sea and led the people through it — verse 13.
He guided them — verse 14.
He brought water out of dry places — verses 15 – 16.
He gave the Israelites everything, but they forgot.

They continued to sin against him, rebelling in the desert against the Most High. They willfully put God to the test by demanding the food they craved.... When the LORD heard them, he was very angry. (verses 17 – 18, 21)

I guess the reason this hit me hard was because it so specifically addresses inappropriate cravings and the reality of how God feels about them. And it just answered so many questions about why this journey has been such a crucial part of my spiritual growth.

My New Year's prayer was, "Unsettle me." In other words, rattle loose my complacent excuses and break apart my stubborn refusals to look, really look at whatever pulls my heart away from God. Even slight tears can weaken the strongest of fabrics.

So ... is there anything I crave besides God?

I know some may shake their heads while thinking I take all this God stuff too seriously.

And I would have to agree completely. I've tasted the deep satisfaction of God and I know all other things are but cheap imitations. And I don't want to be enamored by the lesser things wrought with momentary pleasure.

I've tasted the deep satisfaction of God and I know all other things are but cheap imitations.

I am a woman who has witnessed too much. I am ruined for good.

I too have seen God work miracles.

I've been led through the impossible.

He's guided me.

He's brought living water to replace my dried-up places.

He's given me everything and I don't want to forget.

Not with my mind, not with my soul, not with my heart, and certainly not with my body.

And so I've made the choice to step into a place of intentional sacrifice. A place where my strength would fail, should fail, but hasn't. "My flesh and my heart may fail, but God is the strength of my heart and my portion forever" (Psalm 73:26).

Twenty-six pounds, twenty-five inches ... and a heart empowered by God's strength alone. I have lived this verse as I've pursued to be unsettled, holy, humbled, and filled: "He humbled you, causing you to hunger and then feeding you with manna, which neither you nor your fathers had known, to teach you that man does not live on bread alone but on every word that comes from the mouth of the LORD" (Deuteronomy 8:3).

And I don't want this spiritual journey and the physical victories I've experienced to stop. So, the very next choice I make is a crucial one. Literally, it will determine if I am walking the path of victory or compromise. One wise choice can lead to two, can lead to three, can lead to a thousand, can lead to the sweet place of utter dependence on God and lasting discipline. A place worthy of more than brief vacations every now and then. A place our souls were made to call home.

> *One wise choice can lead to two, can lead to three, can lead to a thousand, can lead to the sweet place of utter dependence on God and lasting discipline.*

A place where discipline makes disciples who truly understand what it means to delight themselves in the Lord. For the Lord has been allowed to rewrite the desires of their hearts. It's a place not wrought with sacrifice but rather a place where they see healthy choices as overflowing blessings so pure and rich, they'd never trade them.

Not for anything.

Especially not for those things they once thought they could never live without.

So, is sustained discipline possible? You tell me. The answer lies within the very next choice you make.

Personal Reflections

1. If you had been in the room with the three pastors Lysa describes at the beginning of the chapter, how would you have answered the question, "Is discipline really sustainable?"

2. Lysa points out the crucial connection between holiness— being set aside for a noble use—and daily disciplines with food (page 168). How do you understand the relationship between your food choices and your ability to "put on the new self, created to be like God in true righteousness and holiness" (Ephesians 4:24)?

3. "The very next choice we make isn't really about the food.... It's about whether or not we're positioning ourselves to live the kind of God-honoring lives in which, by God's strength, sustained discipline is possible" (page 170). Does this idea encourage you or frighten you? Why?

4. Take a moment to reread Lysa's "Unsettle Me" prayer (pages 171–172). Is it a prayer you feel you are ready to pray for yourself? What fears would you have about praying this prayer? What excites you about the possibilities of this prayer for your life?

5. "One wise choice can lead to two, can lead to three, can lead to a thousand, can lead to the sweet place of utter dependence on God and lasting discipline" (page 175). Do you esteem your small, daily food choices or do you tend to feel they don't really matter all that much? How might your life be different if you could achieve utter dependence on God and lasting discipline? What benefits would you most enjoy experiencing?

Things Lost,
Better Things Gained

W e ended the previous chapter with the realization that the very next choice we make is crucially important. This is a great mental perspective to keep. But there's a spiritual perspective we must keep as well. The perspective that we will have to turn from some foods forever. This turning is part courageous sacrifice and part utter repentance. And though the words *sacrifice* and *repentance* used to speak bitter-tasting hardship to my soul, they are speaking something else now. Something I've honestly grown to love. Victory.

But victory won't stay for long if I start resisting and disliking her essential requirements of sacrifice and repentance.

I'm at my goal weight and in the most dangerous place for a dieting success story. Hitting your goal weight is a blessing entangled with a curse. The curse being the assumption that freedom now means returning back to all those things we've given up for the past months. The sacrifices. The missed treats. The deprived taste buds high on salad and low on French fries.

Hitting your goal weight is a blessing entangled with a curse.

It's time to celebrate — live it up — and invite all those foods we've missed so much to a little welcome-home party, right? But we can't welcome home the missed foods without welcoming back all the calories, fat grams, cholesterol, sugars, and addictive additives (think junk food). The interesting thing about these "guests" is that they send out signals to our brain begging us to party with them again and again and again. A little welcome-home party becomes a reinvitation to be roommates, which spells disaster for what we hoped might be lifestyle changes.

Of course, not all diet saboteurs are junk food, but for me even little compromises with unhealthy cravings can quickly pave the road for an all-out reversal of my progress. And this is no longer just a personal revelation; science proves it. In a study recently published by *Science News*, researchers found junk food to be measurably addictive in lab rats:

> After just five days on the junk food diet, rats showed "profound reductions" in the sensitivity of their brains' pleasure centers, suggesting that the animals quickly became habituated to the food. As a result, the rats ate more food to get the same amount of pleasure. Just as heroin addicts require more and more of the drug to feel good, rats needed more and more of the junk food. "They lose control," [one of the researchers] says. "This is the hallmark of addiction."[13]

Other studies I read talked about the effect of certain sugary foods and junk foods that turn off the body's ability to feel full. These studies were complicated and full of chemistry and math terms that made me sweat. My brain is made for stringing words, not chemical equations, so I don't want to delve into lofty science. However, I found it fascinating to see researchers prove by chemistry what I simply call "difficult."

It's really difficult for a chips-and-chocolate girl to uninvite foods to her party that have been regulars for years. And it's even more difficult to reconcile that they aren't my friends. Some can be casual acquaintances on a very limited level, but others need to be banished for good.

Only you can determine which is which. There's a verse we've touched on before in this journey of ours, but it's worth repeating here (it's one I often think about, quote, and try to live the reality of): " 'Everything is permissible for me' — but not everything is beneficial.... I will not be mastered by anything" (1 Corinthians 6:12). Interestingly, most people associate this verse only with sexual sins. However, the very next verse deals with food: " 'Food for the stomach and the stomach for food' — but God will destroy them both" (6:13). Talk about things that make a girl go hmmmmm. The commentary in my Bible remarks about these verses: "Some actions are not sinful in themselves, but they are not appropriate because they can control our lives and lead us away from God."[14]

Food is not the enemy here. Satan is the enemy. And his strategic plan is to render us ineffective or at least sluggish for the cause of Christ. When we're defeated and stuck in issues of the flesh, it's really hard to fully and passionately follow hard after God. So, lest we start mourning what will be lost, we must celebrate all that's being gained through this process.

What if this whole journey of getting healthy could be more about what we're in the process of gaining than what we're losing? In the midst of losing chips and chocolate, there are things to be gained. Things that unleash my weighted down soul, re-inflate my defeated attitude, and set loose a hope that maybe, just maybe, I *can.*

What if this whole journey of getting healthy could be more about what we're in the process of gaining than what we're losing?

I can is a powerful little twist for a girl feeling deprived.

I can helps me walk into the dinner party of my friend and find the conversation more appealing than the buffet. I can helps me stay on the perimeter of the grocery store where the fresher, healthier selections abound and smile that I know this tidbit. I can helps me reach for my water bottle and find satisfaction in its refreshment. I can helps me look at McDonald's drive-thru menu and order a fruit tray without even giving a thought to the Happy Meals I used to "snack" on. I can reminds me to look up a restaurant's nutritional information on the Internet before going out, ensuring wiser choices. I can reminds me no food will ever taste as sweet as victory does.

Today at lunch I threw away most of the sweet potato biscuit that came on the side with my salad entrée. And most of the world's moms gasp and say, "How could you throw away perfectly good food?" Trust me, if it would have been possible to give my biscuit to someone who needs it, I would have in a heartbeat. But in that moment, the very best choice for me was to put the remainder of that biscuit in the trashcan. I'd taken a pinch off the side, enjoyed it immensely, and decided eating the rest would have been overdoing it. And while tossing it, I smiled and said to myself, "This isn't a sign that I'm being deprived. This isn't a trigger for me to pout and say it's not fair. This is a sacrifice I'm willing to make in order to gain something so much greater than the rest of this biscuit. This is the most empowering thing I can do in this moment!" I can. So, I did.

Fellow blogger Anne Jackson wrote a telling post about her weight loss journey when she came to the conclusion early on that there are more things to be gained than just losing weight. And might I say that last sentence just makes me smile. Gaining to lose. Losing to gain. Am I the only one who smiles at things like that?

Anyhow, back to Anne. After her first month of working out and eating healthy, Anne expected big results. But her scale mocked her and made her want to say "words" under her breath. But the way she processed her struggle and the conclusion she reached inspires me for my continued journey. Anne wrote:

Don't trust your scale! One of the things Brandon [her trainer] said to me is most people will attempt working out and eating better for about a month; when they don't see a big difference on the scale, they give up.

Truth be told, if you don't see a big difference on the scale in your first month, it doesn't mean much at all. My scale said, "All this effort and you've only lost a pound," and if I would have believed it, I would have given up.

Don't buy into what the scale says or doesn't say. Trust the effort you are putting into getting healthy. And keep going!

Not only are there changes going on in your body that you can't see, there are changes going on in your spirit — with your discipline, your courage, and your willpower. Keep going![15]

Whether we are at the beginning of our journey, in the middle, or in the danger zone of having just reached our weight loss goals, we can't have a mind-set of this being a hard, impossible sacrifice. Focusing only on what we're giving up will make us feel constantly deprived. And deprivation leads to desperation, frustration, and failure. Instead, we have to focus on everything we're gaining through this process. And see the gains as more valuable than the losses.

Think of an old-fashioned scale. On one side, I place my chips and chocolate and on the other side I place my newfound courage to say "I can." There's no comparison. My courage is so much more valuable and beautiful and empowering and lasting.

Chips and chocolate fill my mouth for a few seconds with a salty and sugary delight that has no life in them. But courage fills my heart, mind, and soul with everything alive and possible and invigorating.

And courage invites me to take one of the hardest steps on a journey like this. Courage says, *Now that you've partially turned from your old habits by making the necessary sacrifices, it's time to fully turn by repenting. Take the step that reads "repentance" and admit your need to stand there a while.* Of all things lost and gained, the courage to repent might just be the most significant for me.

I guess I hadn't really thought of the need to repent until recently. As I finish writing this book, I'm smack dab in the middle of the holidays. So, please excuse me if you are reading this in the midst of summer and feeling very far from all things red, green, light, bright, and jingle bell-ish.

Of all things lost and gained, the courage to repent might just be the most significant for me.

I sat down today to spend a few minutes reading my Bible and decided to read the Christmas story in Mark. I couldn't remember ever reading the Christmas story in that Gospel, so I thought I'd give it a whirl.

Well, it appears Mark believes in cutting to the chase.

There's no mention of a manger. No Mary and Joseph. No baby Jesus. No bright star or angels or heavenly hosts. No silent night. No holy night.

As a matter of fact, if Mark were the only Gospel where Jesus' entrance to this world was mentioned, Christmas would look vastly different.

There would be no gifts.

There would be no Linus delivering the stellar line in the "Charlie Brown" Christmas special.

There would be no lights shining so brightly.

So, what would there be? A wild-looking man named John the Baptist dressed in leather and camel hair, preparing the way for Jesus by preaching one message. A message we don't typically hear at Christmas. A message that's rough around the edges and a little hard to swallow alongside my carrot sticks. Carrot sticks that, just like at the beginning of this book, I still don't crave.

But back to the rough edges of Mark's Christmas message.

Repentance.

That one word sums up the beginnings of Christ's story according to Mark. "And so John came, baptizing in the desert region and preaching a baptism of repentance for the forgiveness of sins. The whole Judean countryside and all the people of Jerusalem went out to him [c]onfessing their sins" (Mark 1:4 – 5).

This is about the place in the sermon where I start hoping some people I know are really paying attention. I climb up on my mental high horse and think, "Thank you, Lord, for this message all these people need to hear because you know how they act. You know how selfish they are. Whew. And you know so-and-so just needs a full-out repentance revival. Mercy!"

It's at that point Jesus whispers to me. *It's a message to you and you alone. You need this message, Lysa. I am calling you to repent. This is the way you need to prepare for Christmas in your heart this year.* "I will send a messenger ahead of you, who will prepare the way — a voice of one calling in the desert, 'Prepare the way for the Lord, make straight paths for him'" (Mark 1:2 – 3).

The girl who can be such a mess.

Hears the messenger calling for repentance.

So, she makes Christmas not the same old story but a message meant for her heart.

And she whispers once again, "I'm sorry, Jesus. Forgive me. Heal me. Restore me. Those little places I excuse. Those same old things that trip me up. The pride that keeps me thinking it's someone else's fault. The busyness that makes me forget to stop and consider my ways, my thoughts, my actions. You, Messiah, are the best match for my mess."

I doubt this will ever be the most popular version of the Christmas story, but for me this year it's perfect. It's a perfect place for this former chips-and-chocolate girl to complete this part of the journey. But not complete as in "I'm finished," so much as complete as in "I'm now perfectly prepared to carry on from here."

Indeed, for me, this has been one of the best spiritual journeys of my life. A significant spiritual journey with great physical benefits.

I have learned so much. But probably one of the richest lessons has been realizing the amount of mental and spiritual energy I wasted for years just wishing things would change. All the while beating myself up for not having the discipline to make those changes.

If you have an issue with weight and food, you know what I mean. But no matter what issue you are currently dealing with, may I offer a bit of encouragement? Jesus wants to help you with that issue. He really does. But you've got to stop beating yourself up about it, determine to follow His lead, and stand in the place of repentance.

We like to identify our shortcomings, form them into a club, and mentally beat the tar out of ourselves. Over and over and over again. We label ourselves and soon lose our real identity to the beaten and bruised fragility we call "me."

How dangerous it is to hold up the intimate knowledge of our imperfections against the outside packaging of others.

We compare, we assume, we assess, we measure, and most times walk away shaking our head at how woefully short our "me" falls when compared to everyone else. How dangerous it is to hold up the intimate knowledge of our imperfections against the outside packaging of others.

If there is one thing that living forty years has taught me, it's this: all God's girls have issues. All of us. Every single one of us. We haul around a bucketload of issues. My issues bucket is probably full of different junk then yours, but it's there nonetheless.

Now, hear me out.

I'm not saying victory isn't possible. It is.

I can make the choice to identify my shortcomings and, instead of using them against myself, hand them over to Jesus and let Him chisel my rough places. The grace-filled way Jesus chisels is so vastly different than the way I beat on myself. My beatings are full of exaggerated lies that defeat. His chiseling is full of truth that sets me free.

Oh, what a difference.

Jesus doesn't compare.

Jesus doesn't condemn.

Jesus doesn't exaggerate.

He simply says, "Hey, I love you. Just as you are. But I love you too much to leave you stuck in this. So, let's fully turn from those things that are not beneficial for you."

I like that about Jesus.

I like that a lot.

I like it more than chips. I like it more than chocolate.

Dear Jesus,

I have finally found the courage to admit I've craved food more than You. I have wept over giving up food while hardly giving a thought to You giving Your life for my freedom. I've been bound up by feelings of helplessness. I've been angry that I have to deal with this weight issue and have been mad at You for allowing this to be one of my lots in life. I've made excuses. I've pointed fingers. I've relied on food for things it could never give me. I've lied to myself about the realities of why I gain weight. I've settled and excused and made pithy comments justifying my issues. I've been enthralled by buttered bread while yawning through Your daily bread.

For all that, I am so sorry. These are not just little issues. These, for me, are sins—missing the mark of Your best for my life. With my whole heart, mind, and soul, I repent. I stand on this step and stare at the reality of my depravity and turn. I turn from the dieting mind-set. I turn from what I must give up and weep no more. I remove my toe keeping open the door to my old habits and patterns, my old mind-set, my old go-to scripts.

I choose freedom. I choose victory. I choose courage. And yes, above all else, I choose You.

> *Amen.*

Personal Reflections

1. "'Everything is permissible for me' — but not everything is beneficial. 'Everything is permissible for me' — but I will not be mastered by anything" (1 Corinthians 6:12). When it comes to healthy eating, what are the things that are permissible for you but not beneficial? Is there anything permissible that might nevertheless have the potential to master you? How do you feel about the idea that you may have to avoid some foods forever?

2. "I can" is a powerful little statement for a girl feeling deprived. In what ways might you incorporate these two very small but mighty words into your healthy eating journey?

3. Think of an old-fashioned balance scale, the kind with a pan on either side that counterbalances one weight against the other. Imagine placing in one pan all the things you need to give up and in the other pan all the things you've gained and will continue to gain. Which side holds the most weight and significance for you?

4. "We like to identify our shortcomings, form them into a club, and mentally beat the tar out of ourselves" (page 184). In what ways have you identified with and punished yourself for your shortcomings? Instead of punishing yourself, can you imagine giving these things to Jesus and asking Him to chisel them away? How might the truth of His compassion help you to break free from your shortcomings in ways that self-condemnation cannot?

Live as an Overcomer

I was standing in the grocery store checkout line last week gazing at rack after rack of magazines that bombarded me with promises of the latest and greatest diet fads. This is such a strange thing, really. The store wants me to buy lots of food, especially the high-profit junk food items. But as I'm paying for my food, the grocery store makes me look at magazines full of models that obviously don't spend a lot of time eating junk food or Paula Dean recipes.

All of the models were a version of thin I'll never know. Their legs were lean and beautifully muscular. Their thighs had avoided the cellulite invasion I've been acquainted with since high school. Their tummies are completely flat. And they looked absolutely stunning in outfits meant for someone who has no body secrets.

Or, maybe their Spanx works a lot better than mine and the graphics artist who airbrushed their cover shot was incredibly generous.

Regardless, I stood there and for the first time realized my mind wasn't racing with self-condemnations. I simply smiled. And I realized my victory isn't tied as much to the way I've changed physically as it is tied to the way I've overcome mentally and spiritually.

Yes, I've lost pounds and inches. But not being weighted down mentally and spiritually by the constant feeling of defeat is the real victory. This freedom and healthy outlook are not tied to what size a person is. There are painfully thin women weighted down spiritually and emotionally by feelings of defeat the same as women many sizes larger than them. I truly think on some level most of us girls struggle with this whole "getting healthy" thing. After all, like I've said before, the very downfall of humanity happened around a circumstance where a woman was tempted with food. So, I do think this is an issue God takes very seriously.

God doesn't just command us to have a healthy perspective on food, He also provides the help to achieve it.

We've seen throughout this journey that God doesn't just command us to have a healthy perspective on food, He also provides the help to achieve it. His Word holds the key for anyone wanting to overcome food issues, be they slight, severe, or anywhere in between. His truths perfectly direct us, guide us, and teach us. And He's proven true to His promises to save us: "Some became fools through their rebellious ways and suffered affliction because of their iniquities. They loathed all food and drew near the gates of death. Then they cried to the LORD in their trouble, and he saved them from their distress" (Psalm 107:17–19).

I relate so much to this passage. You now know my story. I became a fool with my habits regarding food. I rebelled against healthy options, realistic portions, and the need to address this issue in my life. I loved food for the few minutes it took to consume it. But I loathed that same food after overstuffing myself. I suffered afflictions physically, emotionally, and spiritually because of my refusal to admit that food is meant to be consumed by me for my benefit. Food is not meant to consume me to my detriment.

While I can't say I was drawing near to the gates of death physically, I was drawing near to a complete sense of defeat. The way I would secretly beat myself up, haul around loads of guilt, and get mad at God for what seemed like such an unfair curse, was evidence this was a bigger deal than what I dared admit.

When my fellow junk food friends would suddenly find a motivation that eluded me, I responded by getting irritated and grumpy. It can be hard when fellow fat friends get thin. So, I pretended to be perfectly content and justified by quipping, "Whatever. In comparison to a lot of other things I could be doing, this really isn't a big deal. Hand me another brownie, please."

But inside, I was dying. And I was wondering if overcoming this haunting struggle was even remotely possible.

That's an awful place to be.

How precious of God to know and address so specifically a woman's struggle with food. Read this psalm again: "Some became fools through their rebellious ways and suffered affliction because of their iniquities. They loathed all food and drew near the gates of death. Then they cried to the LORD in their trouble, and he saved them from their distress" (Psalm 107:17–19).

And how does He save them?

How does He save the person with issues like mine?

How does He save the anorexic girl who truly loathes all food?

How does He save the severely obese who truly are drawing near to the gates of death?

How does He save any of us acting foolish and rebellious?

The next verse of this same chapter gives the answer: "He sent forth his word and healed them; he rescued them from the grave."

He sent forth His word. And His Word—the Bible—healed them! Can I get some affirmation from the Amen Corner, please?

Jesus girls aren't made to get stuck in a state of defeat.

We aren't.

We were made to walk on paths headed toward victory. This doesn't mean these paths won't be riddled with struggles we'll need to learn to overcome. They will. For lessons on overcoming are some of God's greatest gifts.

Having a weight issue is not God's curse on us.

It is an external manifestation of an internal struggle. Just like debt for the overspender or an overstuffed house for a hoarder, issues with weight are signs that we need to get unstuck from unhealthy habits.

So, God has sent His Word and throughout the pages of this book, I've felt called to really examine God's truths from the vantage point of a girl needing help to get healthy. Not just so all of us can get healthy physically, but so we reach a place of health spiritually and live as overcomers, not victims.

Having a weight issue is not God's curse on us. It is an external manifestation of an internal struggle.

Just the other day I found some of the most fascinating verses about overcoming in the book of Revelation. This is normally a book of the Bible around which I found myself a little skittish; I feel like I should possess a degree of some sorts before knocking on its door. But last week in church the pastor read a verse that intrigued me. So, I flipped to that verse and soon found myself intrigued with many verses.

I was cruising around Revelation like a girl who walks into a store and finds all the mannequins dressed in outfits she can afford and that are exactly what she was hoping to find in her size.

That probably makes no sense to anyone else but me. Who compares reading Revelation to shopping? But what a thrill to find something that fits in so many ways!

Like I said, I have no business trying to comment on verses meant for the halls of a seminary. But on this day, they were meant for simpleminded me on the path of learning to overcome. And I knew it. Check it out: "To him who overcomes, I will give the right to *eat* from the tree of life, which is in the paradise of God" (Revelation 2:7, emphasis added).

We started this journey in Genesis where Eve gave in to her temptation with food. Then, throughout the Old Testament, we found the Israelites, God's people, struggling with food. Remember the lesson God taught them in the desert about dependence on Him by asking for their daily portion of manna? We also found the Psalms rich with verses referencing food. Even in the New Testament book of Philippians God warns us about letting the stomach become an idol in our lives. Now, here we are at the end of the Bible and once again, a pivotal verse about food.

This might be the verse that elicits the greatest excitement in my heart.

To see why, let's read it one more time, then break it apart to unearth the hidden treasure within.

"To him who overcomes, I will give the right to *eat* from the tree of life, which is in the paradise of God" (Revelation 2:7, emphasis added).

Isn't it thrilling to see that overcoming is possible? It is possible to be more than just one who *deals* with their struggles well. This verse says to the one who *overcomes!* In other words, it's for those who find absolute victory in an area where they once knew nothing but defeat.

And there's a reward for pressing through our struggles all the way to absolute victory. Virtually everyone who overcomes will tell you their victory is the sum total of a whole lot of wise decisions, sacrificial decisions, that they made choice by choice, day by day. Yes, knowing a reward awaits us is crucial. And how absolutely tickled I am to know that the reward for overcomers is that they are given the right to *eat!* Eating from the tree of life will be unlike any satisfaction we've ever known. And might I just note that because it specifically says this tree is located in paradise, we will be eating in heaven.

> *Virtually everyone who overcomes will tell you their victory is the sum total of a whole lot of wise decisions that they made day by day.*

Oh, yes we will. Again, Amen Corner, please erupt.

This is why I smiled while standing in that grocery store checkout line I mentioned at the beginning of the chapter. The circumstances were all the same. The magazines were still strategically placed to get my attention. The models were still airbrushed beyond reality. And I still had to buy food.

But my response to all these same circumstances changed because I have changed inside. I have found my "want to" physically, emotionally, and spiritually. My healthy choices make me feel empowered, not deprived. My healthy go-to scripts come so naturally, they aren't rules I follow but the natural way I think about food. And I'm excited about this being my lifestyle. Truly excited.

I hope you are as well. I'll admit, I'm a little sad this book is coming to an end. I have enjoyed walking with you through this journey. But while the book is ending, living out its message is just beginning.

Dare to set your toes firmly on the pathway of victory you are meant to be on. Whether we're on the path toward victory or defeat is determined by the very next choice we make. Not the choices from yesterday. Not the choices five minutes ago.

The next choice. Our very next choice. May it be that of an overcomer. An overcomer made to crave God alone.

Personal Reflections

1. Standing in the checkout line at the grocery store, Lysa experienced a victory she attributes more to mental and spiritual changes than to physical changes. What factors have made the biggest difference in the victories you've experienced with food? Is it food planning? Spiritual disciplines like prayer and dining on the truth of God's Word? Changing your go-to scripts? What things are key to your ongoing success?

2. God's promise in Psalm 107:17 – 20 is that He hears our distress and He heals us with His Word. In what ways would you say God has heard your distress about your struggles with food? What role has Scripture played in helping you to experience God's healing?

3. "To him who overcomes, I will give the right to eat from the tree of life, which is in the paradise of God" (Revelation 2:7). This verse indicates that it's not only possible to overcome our struggles but that there is a reward for those who do — and it involves eating! How might this promise encourage you as you continue on your healthy eating adventure?

Verses by Chapter

These verses either appear in the chapter or are applicable to the subject matter of the chapter.

CHAPTER 1: **What's Really Going On Here?**

Psalm 84:1-2

> How lovely is your dwelling place, O LORD Almighty! My soul yearns, event faints, for the courts of the LORD; my heart and my flesh cry out for the living God.

1 John 2:15-16

> Do not love the world or anything in the world. If anyone loves the world, the love of the Father is not in him. For everything in the world—the cravings of sinful man, the lust of his eyes and the boasting of what he has and does—comes not from the Father but from the world.

Genesis 3:6

> When the woman saw that the fruit of the tree was good for food and pleasing to the eye, and also desirable for gaining wisdom, she took some and ate it.

Matthew 4:1-11

> Then Jesus was led by the Spirit into the desert to be tempted by the devil. After fasting forty days and forty nights, he was hungry.

The tempter came to him and said, "If you are the Son of God, tell these stones to become bread." Jesus answered, "It is written: 'Man does not live on bread alone, but on every word that comes from the mouth of God.'" Then the devil took him to the holy city and had him stand on the highest point of the temple. "If you are the Son of God," he said, "throw yourself down. For it is written: 'He will command his angels concerning you, and they will lift you up in their hands, so that you will not strike your foot against a stone.'" Jesus answered him, "It is also written: 'Do not put the Lord your God to the test.'" Again, the devil took him to a very high mountain and showed him all the kingdoms of the world and their splendor. "All this I will give you," he said, "if you will bow down and worship me." Jesus said to him, "Away from me, Satan! For it is written: 'Worship the Lord your God, and serve him only.'" Then the devil left him, and angels came and attended him.

CHAPTER 2: Replacing My Cravings

Psalm 78:18

They willfully put God to the test by demanding the food they craved.

Psalm 5:1–3

Give ear to my words, O LORD, consider my sighing. Listen to my cry for help, my King and my God, for to you I pray. In the morning, O LORD, you hear my voice; in the morning I lay my requests before you and wait in expectation.

CHAPTER 3: Getting a Plan

Luke 8:15

But the seed on good soil stands for those with a noble and good heart, who hear the word, retain it, and by persevering produce a crop.

Isaiah 43:18 – 19

Forget the former things; do not dwell on the past. See, I am doing a new thing! Now it springs up; do you not perceive it? I am making a way in the desert and streams in the wasteland.

Psalm 34:4 – 8

I sought the LORD, and he answered me; he delivered me from all my fears. Those who look to him are radiant; their faces are never covered with shame. This poor man called, and the LORD heard him; he saved him out of all his troubles. The angel of the LORD encamps around those who fear him, and he delivers them. Taste and see that the LORD is good; blessed is the man who takes refuge in him.

CHAPTER 4: Friends Don't Let Friends Eat before Thinking

Ecclesiastes 4:9 – 10, 12

Two are better than one, because they have a good return for their work: If one falls down, his friend can help him up. But pity the man who falls and has no one to help him up! ... Though one may be overpowered, two can defend themselves. A cord of three strands is not quickly broken.

Genesis 25:29 – 31, 33 – 34

Once when Jacob was cooking some stew, Esau came in from the open country, famished. He said to Jacob, "Quick, let me have some of that red stew!" ... Jacob replied, "First, sell me your birthright." ... So [Esau] swore an oath to him, selling his birthright to Jacob [for] some bread and some lentil stew.

CHAPTER 5: Made for More

Ephesians 1:17 – 20

I keep asking that the God of our Lord Jesus Christ, the glorious Father, may give you the Spirit of wisdom and revelation, so that you may know him better. I pray also that the eyes of your heart may be enlightened in order that you may know the hope to which he has called you, the riches of his glorious inheritance in the saints, and his incomparably great power for us who believe. That power is like the working of his mighty strength, which he exerted in Christ when he raised him from the dead and seated him at his right hand in the heavenly realms.

Romans 3:24

[We] are justified freely by his grace through the redemption that came by Christ Jesus.

Romans 8:1 – 2

Therefore, there is now no condemnation for those who are in Christ Jesus, because through Christ Jesus the law of the Spirit of life set me free from the law of sin and death.

1 Corinthians 1:2

To the church of God in Corinth, to those sanctified in Christ Jesus and called to be holy, together with all those everywhere who call on the name of our Lord Jesus Christ — their Lord and ours.

1 Corinthians 1:30

It is because of him that you are in Christ Jesus, who has become for us wisdom from God — that is, our righteousness, holiness and redemption.

2 Corinthians 5:17

Therefore, if anyone is in Christ, he is a new creation; the old has gone, the new has come!

Ephesians 1:4

For he chose us in him before the creation of the world to be holy and blameless in his sight.

Ephesians 2:13

But now in Christ Jesus you who once were far away have been brought near through the blood of Christ.

Ephesians 3:12

In him and through faith in him we may approach God with freedom and confidence.

Romans 8:37

No, in all these things we are more than conquerors through him who loved us.

CHAPTER 6: **Growing Closer to God**

Luke 9:23

Then he said to them all: "If anyone would come after me, he must deny himself and take up his cross daily and follow me."

Galatians 5:22–23

But the fruit of the Spirit is love, joy, peace, patience, kindness, goodness, faithfulness, gentleness and self-control.

Galatians 5:16

So I say, live by the Spirit, and you will not gratify the desires of the sinful nature.

Romans 8:11

And if the Spirit of him who raised Jesus from the dead is living in you, he who raised Christ from the dead will also give life to your mortal bodies through his Spirit, who lives in you.

Galatians 5:25

Since we live by the Spirit, let us keep in step with the Spirit.

John 4:34

"My food," said Jesus, "is to do the will of him who sent me and to finish his work."

Philippians 3:13 – 16

But one thing I do: Forgetting what is behind and straining toward what is ahead, I press on toward the goal to win the prize for which God has called me heavenward in Christ Jesus. All of us who are mature should take such a view of things. And if on some point you think differently, that too God will make clear to you. Only let us live up to what we have already attained.

Philippians 3:18 – 19

For, as I have often told you before and now say again even with tears, many live as enemies of the cross of Christ. Their destiny is destruction, their god is their stomach, and their glory is in their shame. Their mind is on earthly things.

Philippians 3:20 – 21

But our citizenship is in heaven. And we eagerly await a Savior from there, the Lord Jesus Christ, who, by the power that enables him to bring everything under his control, will transform our lowly bodies so that they will be like his glorious body.

CHAPTER 7: I'm Not Defined by the Numbers

Isaiah 45:23

I will go before you and will level the mountains; I will break down gates of bronze and cut through bars of iron. I will give you the treasures of darkness, riches stored in secret places, so that you may know that I am the LORD, the God of Israel, who summons you by name.

2 Peter 1:3 – 11

His divine power has given us everything we need for life and godliness through our knowledge of him who called us by his own glory and goodness. Through these he has given us his very great and precious promises, so that through them you may participate in the divine nature and escape the corruption in the world caused by evil desires. For this very reason, make every effort to add to your faith goodness; and to goodness, knowledge; and to knowledge, self-control; and to self-control, perseverance; and to perseverance, godliness; and to godliness, brotherly kindness; and to brotherly kindness, love. For if you possess these qualities in increasing measure, they will keep you from being ineffective and unproductive in your knowledge of our Lord Jesus Christ. But if anyone does not have them, he is nearsighted and blind, and has forgotten that he has been cleansed from his past sins. Therefore, my brothers, be all the more eager to make your calling and election sure. For if you do these things, you will never fall, and you will receive a rich welcome into the eternal kingdom of our Lord and Savior Jesus Christ.

2 Corinthians 10:5

We demolish arguments and every pretension that sets itself up against the knowledge of God, and we take captive every thought to make it obedient to Christ.

1 Thessalonians 2:12

... encouraging, comforting and urging you to live lives worthy of God, who calls you into his kingdom and glory.

2 Corinthians 7:1

Since we have these promises, dear friends, let us purify ourselves from everything that contaminates body and spirit, perfecting holiness out of reverence for God.

Ephesians 5:26

... to make her holy, cleansing her by the washing with water through the word.

CHAPTER 8: Making Peace with the Realities of My Body

Psalm 103:1–5

Praise the LORD, O my soul; all my inmost being, praise his holy name. Praise the LORD, O my soul, and forget not all his benefits — who forgives all your sins and heals all your diseases, who redeems your life from the pit and crowns you with love and compassion, who satisfies your desires with good things so that your youth is renewed like the eagle's.

Ephesians 2:10

For we are God's workmanship, created in Christ Jesus to do good works, which God prepared in advance for us to do.

2 Corinthians 4:16

Therefore we do not lose heart. Though outwardly we are wasting away, yet inwardly we are being renewed day by day.

Romans 12:1–8

Therefore, I urge you, brothers, in view of God's mercy, to offer your bodies as living sacrifices, holy and pleasing to God — this is your spiritual act of worship. Do not conform any longer to the pattern of this world, but be transformed by the renewing of your mind. Then you will be able to test and approve what God's will is — his good, pleasing and perfect will. For by the grace given me I say to every one of you: Do not think of yourself more highly than you ought, but rather think of yourself with sober judgment, in accordance with the measure of faith God has given you. Just as each of us has one body with many members, and these members do not all have the same function, so in Christ we who are many form one body, and each member belongs to all the others. We have different gifts, according to the grace given us. If a man's gift is prophesying, let him use it in proportion to his faith. If it is serving, let him serve; if it is teaching, let him teach; if it is encouraging, let him encourage; if it is contributing to the needs of others, let him give generously; if it is leadership, let him govern diligently; if it is showing mercy, let him do it cheerfully.

CHAPTER 9: But Exercise Makes Me Want to Cry

Psalm 73:26

My flesh and my heart may fail, but God is the strength of my heart and my portion forever.

Psalm 86:11 – 12

Teach me your way, O LORD, and I will walk in your truth; give me an undivided heart, that I may fear your name. I will praise you, O LORD my God, with all my heart; I will glorify your name forever.

1 Corinthians 6:19 – 20

Do you not know that your body is a temple of the Holy Spirit, who is in you, whom you have received from God? You are not your own; you were bought at a price. Therefore honor God with your body.

Haggai 1:2 – 8

This is what the LORD Almighty says: "These people say, 'The time has not yet come for the LORD's house to be built.'" Then the word of the LORD came through the prophet Haggai: "Is it a time for you yourselves to be living in your paneled houses, while this house remains a ruin?" Now this is what the LORD Almighty says: "Give careful thought to your ways. You have planted much, but have harvested little. You eat, but never have enough. You drink, but never have your fill. You put on clothes, but are not warm. You earn wages, only to put them in a purse with holes in it." This is what the LORD Almighty says: "Give careful thought to your ways. Go up into the mountains and bring down timber and build the house, so that I may take pleasure in it and be honored," says the LORD.

Ezekiel 6:9 – 10

[H]ow I have been grieved by their adulterous hearts, which have turned away from me, and by their eyes which have lusted after their idols. They will loathe themselves for the evil they have done and for all their detestable practices. And they will know that I am the LORD; I did not threaten in vain to bring this calamity on them.

Psalm 90:12

Teach us to number our days aright, that we may gain a heart of wisdom.

Psalm 39:4

Show me, O LORD, my life's end and the number of my days; let me know how fleeting is my life.

Psalm 40:8

I desire to do your will, O my God; your law is within my heart.

Hebrews 12:1

Therefore, since we are surrounded by such a great cloud of witnesses, let us throw off everything that hinders and the sin that so easily entangles, and let us run with perseverance the race marked out for us.

CHAPTER 10: **This Isn't Fair!**

2 Corinthians 12:9 – 10

But he said to me, "My grace is sufficient for you, for my power is made perfect in weakness." Therefore I will boast all the more gladly about my weaknesses, so that Christ's power may rest on me. That is why, for Christ's sake, I delight in weaknesses, in insults, in hardships, in persecutions, in difficulties. For when I am weak, then I am strong.

James 1:2 – 4

Consider it pure joy, my brothers, whenever you face trials of many kinds, because you know that the testing of your faith develops perseverance. Perseverance must finish its work so that you may be mature and complete, not lacking anything.

1 Peter 5:6 – 10

Humble yourselves, therefore, under God's mighty hand, that he may lift you up in due time. Cast all your anxiety on him because he cares for you. Be self-controlled and alert. Your enemy the devil prowls like a roaring lion looking for someone to devour. Resist him, standing firm in the faith, because you know that your brothers throughout the world are undergoing the same kind of sufferings. And the God of all grace, who called you to his eternal glory in Christ, after you have suffered a little while, will himself restore you and make you strong, firm and steadfast.

CHAPTER 11: Stinkin', Rotten, Horrible, No Good Day

Deuteronomy 2:3 (NASB)

You have circled this mountain long enough. Now turn north.

Romans 8:26

In the same way, the Spirit helps us in our weakness. We do not know what we ought to pray for, but the Spirit himself intercedes for us with groans that words cannot express.

Ephesians 3:17 – 19

And I pray that you, being rooted and established in love, may have power, together with all the saints, to grasp how wide and long and high and deep is the love of Christ, and to know this love that surpasses knowledge — that you may be filled to the measure of all the fullness of God.

1 John 3:1

How great is the love the Father has lavished on us, that we should be called children of God! And that is what we are!

Psalm 103:17

But from everlasting to everlasting the LORD's love is with those who fear him.

Romans 8:38 – 39

For I am convinced that neither death nor life, neither angels nor demons, neither the present nor the future, nor any powers, neither height nor depth, nor anything else in all creation, will be able to separate us from the love of God that is in Christ Jesus our Lord.

Psalm 89:2

I will declare that your love stands firm forever, that you established your faithfulness in heaven itself.

1 John 4:9

This is how God showed his love among us: He sent his one and only Son into the world that we might live through him.

Romans 5:5

And hope does not disappoint us, because God has poured out his love into our hearts by the Holy Spirit, whom he has given us.

Psalm 103:8

The LORD is compassionate and gracious, slow to anger, abounding in love.

1 John 2:5

But if anyone obeys his word, God's love is truly made complete in him. This is how we know we are in him.

Revelation 3:8

See, I have placed before you an open door that no one can shut.

1 Thessalonians 2:13

And we also thank God continually because, when you received the word of God, which you heard from us, you accepted it not as the word of men, but as it actually is, the word of God, which is at work in you who believe.

Hebrews 2:14, 18

Since the children have flesh and blood, he too shared in their humanity so that by his death he might destroy him who holds the power of death—that is, the devil.... Because he himself suffered when he was tempted, he is able to help those who are being tempted.

Hebrews 3:1

Therefore, holy brothers, who share in the heavenly calling, fix your thoughts on Jesus, the apostle and high priest whom we confess.

CHAPTER 12: The Curse of the Skinny Jeans

John 15:9 - 12

As the Father has loved me, so I have loved you. Now remain in my love. If you obey my commands, you will remain in my love, just as I have obeyed my Father's commands and remain in his love. I have told you this so that my joy may be in you and that your joy may be complete. My command is this: Love each other as I have loved you.

Isaiah 55:8 - 12

"For my thoughts are not your thoughts, neither are your ways my ways," declares the LORD. "As the heavens are higher than the earth, so are my ways higher than your ways and my thoughts than your thoughts. As the rain and the snow come down from heaven, and do not return to it without watering the earth and making it bud and flourish, so that it yields seed for the sower and bread for the eater, so is my word that goes out from my mouth: It will not return to me empty, but will accomplish what I desire and achieve the purpose for which I sent it. You will go out in joy and be led forth in peace."

James 1:2 - 4

Consider it pure joy, my brothers, whenever you face trails of many kinds, because you know that the testing of your faith develops perseverance. Perseverance must finish its work so that you may be mature and complete, not lacking anything.

CHAPTER 13: Overindulgence

Proverbs 23:20 - 21

Do not join those who drink too much wine or gorge themselves on meat, for drunkards and gluttons become poor, and drowsiness clothes them in rags.

Proverbs 28:7

He who keeps the law is a discerning son, but a companion of gluttons disgraces his father.

Psalm 42:1 - 2

As the deer pants for streams of water, so my soul pants for you, O God. My soul thirsts for God, for the living God. When can I go and meet with God?

Psalm 143:6

I spread out my hands to you; my soul thirsts for you like a parched land.

Exodus 16:2 - 4

In the desert the whole community grumbled against Moses and Aaron. The Israelites said to them, "If only we had died by the LORD's hand in Egypt! There we sat around pots of meat and ate all the food we wanted, but you have brought us out into this desert to starve this entire assembly to death." Then the LORD said to Moses, "I will rain down bread from heaven for you. The people are to go out each day and gather enough for that day. In this way I will test them and see whether they will follow my instructions."

Lamentations 3:22 – 24

Because of the LORD's great love we are not consumed, for his compassions never fail. They are new every morning; great is your faithfulness. I say to myself, "The LORD is my portion; therefore I will wait for him."

Psalm 107:9

For he satisfies the thirsty and fills the hungry with good things.

CHAPTER 14: Emotional Emptiness

Philippians 4:8

Whatever is true, whatever is noble, whatever is right, whatever is pure, whatever is lovely, whatever is admirable—if anything is excellent or praiseworthy—think about such things.

Ecclesiastes 3:11

He has made everything beautiful in its time. He has also set eternity in the hearts of men; yet they cannot fathom what God has done from beginning to end.

CHAPTER 15: The Demon in the Chips Poster

Psalm 106:14

In the desert they gave in to their craving; in the wasteland they put God to the test.

CHAPTER 16: Why Diets Don't Work

1 Corinthians 10:12 – 14

So, if you think you are standing firm, be careful that you don't fall! No temptation has seized you except what is common to man. And God is faithful; he will not let you be tempted beyond what you can bear. But when you are tempted, he will provide a way out so that you can stand up under it. Therefore, my dear friends, flee from idolatry.

Colossians 2:20 – 23

Since you died with Christ to the basic principles of this world, why, as though you still belonged to it, do you submit to its rules: "Do not handle! Do not taste! Do not touch!"? These are all destined to perish with use, because they are based on human commands and teachings. Such regulations indeed have an appearance of wisdom, with their self-imposed worship, their false humility and their harsh treatment of the body, but they lack any value in restraining sensual indulgence.

2 Corinthians 6:16

What agreement is there between the temple of God and idols? For we are the temple of the living God. As God has said: "I will live with them and walk among them, and I will be their God, and they will be my people."

CHAPTER 17: The Very Next Choice We Make

2 Corinthians 7:1

Since we have these promises, dear friends, let us purify ourselves from everything that contaminates body and spirit, perfecting holiness out of reverence for God.

Ephesians 4:22 – 24

You were taught, with regard to your former way of life, to put off your old self, which is being corrupted by its deceitful desires; to be made new in the attitude of your minds; and to put on the new self, created to be like God in true righteousness and holiness.

Romans 6:19

I put this in human terms because you are weak in your natural selves. Just as you used to offer the parts of your body in slavery to impurity and to ever-increasing wickedness, so now offer them in slavery to righteousness leading to holiness.

Psalm 78:12 - 18

He did miracles in the sight of their fathers in the land of Egypt, in the region of Zoan. He divided the sea and led them through; he made the water stand firm like a wall. He guided them with the cloud by day and with light from the fire all night. He split the rocks in the desert and gave them water as abundant as the seas; he brought streams out of a rocky crag and made water flow down like rivers. But they continued to sin against him, rebelling in the desert against the Most High. They willfully put God to the test by demanding the food they craved.

Psalm 78:21

When the Lord heard them, he was very angry; his fire broke out against Jacob, and his wrath rose against Israel.

Psalm 73:26

My flesh and my heart may fail, but God is the strength of my heart and my portion forever.

Deuteronomy 8:3

He humbled you, causing you to hunger and then feeding you with manna, which neither you nor your fathers had known, to teach you that man does not live on bread alone but on every word that comes from the mouth of the LORD.

James 1:12 - 25

Blessed is the man who perseveres under trial, because when he has stood the test, he will receive the crown of life that God has promised to those who love him. When tempted, no one should say, "God is tempting me." For God cannot be tempted by evil, nor does he tempt anyone; but each one is tempted when, by his own evil desire, he is dragged away and enticed. Then, after desire has conceived, it gives birth to sin; and sin, when it is full-grown, gives birth to death. Don't be deceived, my dear brothers. Every good and perfect gift is from above, coming down from the Father of the heavenly lights, who does not change like shifting shadows. He chose to give us birth through the word of truth, that we might be a kind of firstfruits of all he created. My dear brothers, take note of this: Everyone should be quick to listen, slow to speak and slow to become angry, for man's anger does not bring about the righteous life that God desires. Therefore, get rid of all moral filth and the evil that is so prevalent and humbly accept the word planted in you, which can save you. Do not merely listen to the word, and so deceive yourselves. Do what it says. Anyone who listens to the word but does not do what it says is like a man who looks at his face in a mirror and, after looking at himself, goes away and immediately forgets what he looks like. But the man who looks intently into the perfect law that gives freedom, and continues to do this, not forgetting what he has heard, but doing it — he will be blessed in what he does.

1 Thessalonians 5:23

May God himself, the God of peace, sanctify you through and through. May your whole spirit, soul and body be kept blameless at the coming of our Lord Jesus Christ.

CHAPTER 18: Things Lost, Better Things Gained

1 Corinthians 6:12

"Everything is permissible for me" — but not everything is beneficial.... I will not be mastered by anything.

Mark 1:2-5

"I will send a messenger ahead of you, who will prepare the way — a voice of one calling in the desert, 'Prepare the way for the Lord, make straight paths for him.'" And so John came, baptizing in the desert region and preaching a baptism of repentance for the forgiveness of sins. The whole Judean countryside and all the people of Jerusalem went out to him [c]onfessing their sins.

CHAPTER 19: **Live as an Overcomer**

Psalm 107:17-19

Some became fools through their rebellious ways and suffered affliction because of their iniquities. They loathed all food and drew near the gates of death. Then they cried to the LORD in their trouble, and he saved them from their distress.

Revelation 2:4

Yet I hold this against you: You have forsaken your first love.

Revelation 2:5

Remember the height from which you have fallen! Repent and do the things you did at first.

Revelation 2:7

To him who overcomes, I will give the right to eat from the tree of life, which is in the paradise of God.

Isaiah 58:8-9, 11

Then your light will break forth like the dawn, and your healing will quickly appear; then your righteousness will go before you, and the glory of the LORD will be your rear guard. Then you will call, and the LORD will answer; you will cry for help, and he will say: Here am I.... The LORD will guide you always; he will satisfy your needs in a sun-scorched land and will strengthen your frame. You will be like a well-watered garden, like a spring whose waters never fail.

Healthy Eating
Go-To Scripts

1. God has given me power over my food choices. I'm supposed to consume food. *Food isn't supposed to consume me.*

> But he said to me, "My grace is sufficient for you, for my power is made perfect in weakness."... For when I am weak, then I am strong. (2 Corinthians 12:9–10)

2. *I was made for more* than to be stuck in a vicious cycle of defeat.

> You have circled this mountain long enough. Now turn north. (Deuteronomy 2:3 NASB)

3. When I am considering a compromise, I will think past this moment and ask myself, *How will I feel about this choice tomorrow morning?*

> Do you not know that your body is a temple of the Holy Spirit, who is in you, whom you have received from God? You are not your own; you were bought at a price. Therefore honor God with your body. (1 Corinthians 6:19–20)

4. When tempted, I either *remove the temptation* or *remove myself* from the situation.

> So, if you think you are standing firm, be careful that you don't fall! No temptation has seized you except what is

common to man. And God is faithful; he will not let you be tempted beyond what you can bear. But when you are tempted, he will also provide a way out so that you can stand up under it. Therefore, my dear friends, flee. (1 Corinthians 10:12 – 14)

5. When there's a special event, I can find *other ways to celebrate* rather than blowing my healthy eating plan.

See, I have placed before you an open door that no one can shut. (Revelation 3:8)

6. *Struggling with my weight isn't God's mean curse on me*, but an outside indication that internal changes are needed for me to function and feel well.

Forget the former things; do not dwell on the past. See, I am doing a new thing!... I am making a way in the desert and streams in the wasteland. (Isaiah 43:18 – 19)

7. I have these boundaries in place *not for restriction* but rather to *define the parameters of my freedom.*

I put this in human terms because you are weak in your natural selves. Just as you used to offer the parts of your body in slavery to impurity and to ever-increasing wickedness, so now offer them in slavery to righteousness leading to holiness. (Romans 6:19)

Notes

1. http://www.pubmedcentral.nih.gov/articlerender.fcgi?artid=1856611

2. http://dictionary.reference.com/browse/craving

3. http://dictionary.reference.com/browse/enlightened

4. Used by permission of Karen Ehman. You can find this post on her delightful blog at: http://karenehman.com/home/2009/10/28/defined-by-obedience-not-by-a-number-and-a-giveaway/

5. Inspirational Quotes on Beauty collected by Maddie Ruud: http://hubpages.com/hub/Quotes_on_Beauty

6. Ruth Graham, *Fear Not Tomorrow, God Is Already There* (New York: Howard Books, 2009), 104–5.

7. Bob Greene, *The Best Life Diet* (New York: Simon and Schuster, 2006). In the foreword by Oprah Winfrey, 15–16.

8. http://cougar.eb.com/dictionary/gluttony

9. Chip Ingram, *The Invisible War* (Grand Rapids: Baker, 2006), 27.

10. http://www.cswd.org/docs/ltdietstudy.html and http://jama.amaassn.org/cgi/content/abstract/289/14/1792?etoc

11. Ray Stedman, "The Things That Can Ruin Your Faith," message on Colossians 2:16–23 delivered January 25, 1987, http://www.raystedman.org

12. Dr. Chilton's latest book, *The Gene Smart Diet*, was published in July 2009. This quote was taken from "Help, I Can't Stop Eating," an article in the *US Airways In Flight* magazine (June–July 2009). http://www.usairwaysmag.com/articles/help_i_cant_stop_eating/

13. http://www.sciencenews.org/view/generic/id/48605/title/Junk_food_turns_rats_into_addicts

14. *Life Application Study Bible (NIV)* footnote for 1 Corinthians 6:12 (Grand Rapids: Zondervan, 2004), 2070.

15. http://flowerdust.net/2009/12/17/what-the-scale-didnt-say/

About Lysa TerKeurst

Lysa TerKeurst is a wife to Art and mom to five priority blessings named Jackson, Mark, Hope, Ashley, and Brooke. The author of more than a dozen books, she has been featured on *Focus on the Family*, *Good Morning America*, the *Oprah Winfrey Show*, and in *O Magazine*. Her greatest passion is inspiring women to say yes to God and take part in the awesome adventure He has designed every soul to live. While she is the cofounder of Proverbs 31 Ministries, to those who know her best she is simply a car-pooling mom who loves her family, loves Jesus passionately, and struggles like the rest of us with laundry, junk drawers, and cellulite.

WEBSITE: If you enjoyed this book by Lysa, you'll love all the additional resources found at *www.MadetoCrave.org*.

BLOG: Dialog with Lysa through her daily blog, see pictures of her family, and follow her speaking schedule. She'd love to meet you at an event in your area! *www.Lysa TerKeurst.com*.

BOOKING LYSA TO SPEAK: If you are interested in booking Lysa for a speaking engagement, contact Holly Good: *Holly@Proverbs31.org*.

A Gift Just for You

Get this free colorful magnet to keep you inspired and on track. The only charge is $1.00 for shipping and handling. Place your order by emailing: *Resources@Proverbs31 .org* and put "Made to Crave Magnet" in the subject line. Bulk orders for Bible studies and small groups are also available with special shipping rates.

To download other free inspirational sayings, be sure to visit *www.MadetoCrave.org*, where you'll find many additional resources.

About Proverbs 31 Ministries

If you were inspired by *Made to Crave* and yearn to deepen your own personal relationship with Jesus Christ, I encourage you to connect with Proverbs 31 Ministries. Proverbs 31 Ministries exists to be a trusted friend who will take you by the hand and walk by your side, leading you one step closer to the heart of God through:

- *Encouragement for Today*, free online daily devotions
- The *P31 Woman* monthly magazine
- Daily radio program

To learn more about Proverbs 31 Ministries or to inquire about having Lysa TerKeurst speak at your event, contact Holly Good (*Holly@Proverbs31.org*), or visit *www.Proverbs31.org*.

Proverbs 31 Ministries
616-G Matthews-Mint Hill Road
Matthews, NC 28105
www.Proverbs31.org

Made to Crave
DVD Curriculum

Satisfying Your Deepest Desire with God, Not Food

Lysa TerKeurst
President of Proverbs 31 Ministries

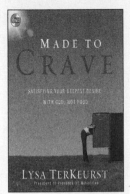

According to author Lysa TerKeurst, craving isn't a bad thing, but we must realize God created us to crave so we'd ultimately desire more of Him in our lives. Many of us have misplaced that craving, overindulging in physical pleasures instead of lasting spiritual satisfaction.

For a woman struggling with unhealthy eating habits, *Made to Crave* will equip her to:

- Break the "I'll start again Monday cycle" and start feeling good about herself today
- Stop beating herself up over the numbers on the scale and make peace with the body she's been given
- Discover how weight loss struggles aren't a curse but, rather, a blessing in the making
- Replace justifications that lead to diet failure with empowering go-to scripts that lead to victory
- Eat healthy without feeling deprived
- Reach a healthy weight goal while growing closer to God in the process

Made to Crave session titles include:

Session 1: From Deprivation to Empowerment

Session 2: From Desperation to Determination

Session 3: From Guilt to Peace

Session 4: From Triggers to Truth

Session 5: From Permissible to Beneficial

Session 6: From Consumed to Courageous

Bonus Session: Moving the Mountain

The *Made to Crave* DVD is designed for use with the *Made to Crave Participant's Guide*.

Becoming More Than a Good Bible Study Girl

Lysa TerKeurst, President of Proverbs 31 Ministries

Is Something Missing in Your Life?

Lysa TerKeurst knows what it's like to consider God just another thing on her to-do list. For years she went through the motions of a Christian life: Go to church. Pray. Be nice.

Longing for a deeper connection between what she knew in her head and her everyday reality, she wanted to personally experience God's presence.

Drawing from her own remarkable story of step-by-step faith, Lysa invites you to uncover the spiritually exciting life we all yearn for. With her trademark wit and spiritual wisdom, Lysa will help you :

- Learn how to make a Bible passage come alive in your own devotion time.
- Replace doubt, regret, and envy with truth, confidence, and praise.
- Stop the unhealthy cycles of striving and truly learn to love who you are and what you've been given.
- Discover how to have inner peace and security in any situation.
- Sense God responding to your prayers.

The adventure God has in store for your life just might blow you away.

Available in stores and online!

ZONDERVAN®
.com

Becoming More Than a Good Bible Study Girl DVD Curriculum

Living the Faith after Bible Class Is Over

Lysa TerKeurst, President of Proverbs 31 Ministries

"I really want to know God, personally and intimately."

Those words of speaker, award-winning author, and popular blogger Lysa TerKeurst mirror the feelings of countless women. They're tired of just going through the motions of being a Christian: Go to church. Pray. Be nice. That spiritual to-do list just doesn't cut it. But what does? How can ordinary, busy moms, wives, and workers step out of the drudgery of religious duty to experience a living, moment-by-moment, deeply intimate relationship with God?

In six small group DVD sessions designed for use with the *Becoming More Than a Good Bible Study Girl Participant's Guide*, Lysa shows women how they can transform their walk with God from lackluster theory to vibrant reality. The *Becoming More Than a Bible Study Girl* DVD curriculum guides participants on an incredible, tremendously rewarding journey on which they will discover how to:

- Build personal, two-way conversations with God.
- Study the Bible and experience life-change for themselves.
- Cultivate greater authenticity and depth in their relationships.
- Make disappointments work for them, not against them.
- Find incredible joy as they live out their faith in everyday circumstances.

Available in stores and online!

ZONDERVAN®
.com

Share Your Thoughts

With the Author: Your comments will be forwarded to the author when you send them to *zauthor@zondervan.com*.

With Zondervan: Submit your review of this book by writing to *zreview@zondervan.com*.

Free Online Resources at

www.zondervan.com

Zondervan AuthorTracker: Be notified whenever your favorite authors publish new books, go on tour, or post an update about what's happening in their lives at www.zondervan.com/authortracker.

Daily Bible Verses and Devotions: Enrich your life with daily Bible verses or devotions that help you start every morning focused on God. Visit www.zondervan.com/newsletters.

Free Email Publications: Sign up for newsletters on Christian living, academic resources, church ministry, fiction, children's resources, and more. Visit www.zondervan.com/newsletters.

Zondervan Bible Search: Find and compare Bible passages in a variety of translations at www.zondervanbiblesearch.com.

Other Benefits: Register yourself to receive online benefits like coupons and special offers, or to participate in research.